CW00833456

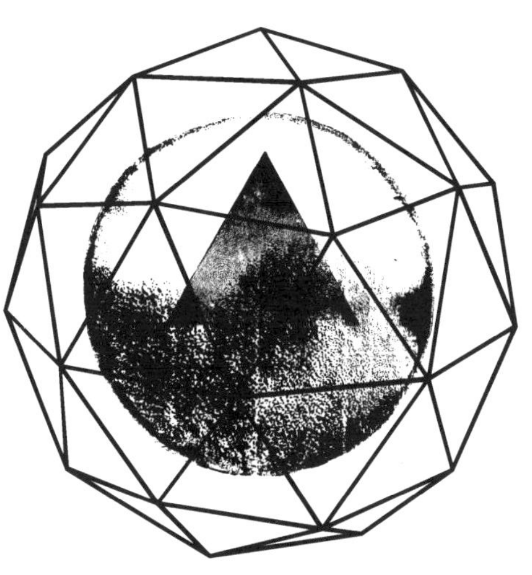

BOOKS BY GUILLAUME WOLF "PROF. G"

- *You Are a Quest*
- *You Are a Dream*
- *You Are a Message*
- *You Are a Circle*
- *Super Hyper Vibe!*

For information about the author, workshops, and additional content, please visit **www.ProfG.co**

SUPER HYPER VIBE!

THE MODERN GUIDEBOOK FOR YOUR SOUL'S AWAKENING
[A REUNION PRIMER]

GUILLAUME WOLF "PROF. G"

FIRST EDITION

Texts, photos, and woodblock art: Guillaume Wolf.
Sacred geometry vectors: Skybox Creative.
Cat: Eadweard Muybridge, *a cat running,* 1887.

Copy editor: Kristin M. Jones.

For the sleepers

who found the courage

to open their eyes

and wake up

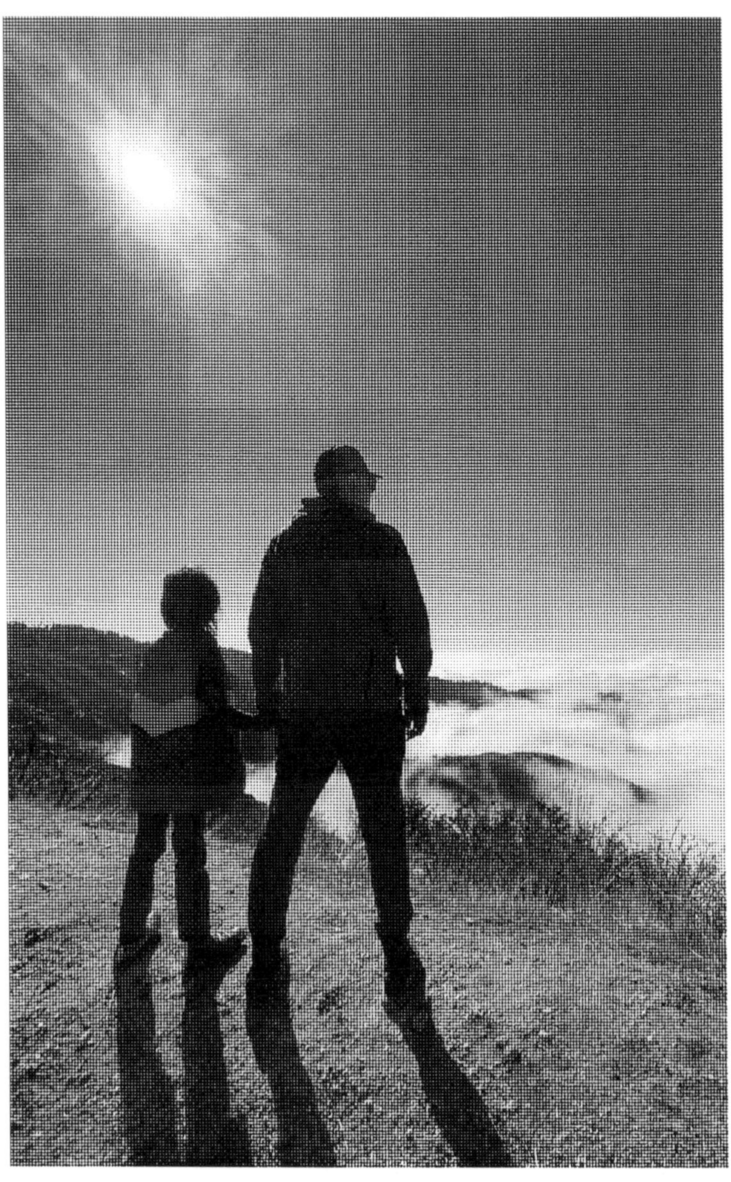

The author with his daughter, San Bernardino Mountains, California.

I went to the woods because I wished to live deliberately, to front only the essential facts of life, and see if I could not learn what it had to teach, and not, when I came to die, discover that I had not lived.

— **Henry David Thoreau**

You must understand the whole of life, not just one little part of it. That is why you must read, that is why you must look at the skies, that is why you must sing and dance, and write poems and suffer and understand, for all that is life.

— **Jiddu Krishnamurti**

As I understand it, the work of the philosopher as artist is to reveal and celebrate the eternal.

— **Alan Watts**

TABLE OF CONTENTS

A LETTER FOR YOU

Welcome, my creative, seeker friend!

I hope you are well.

Here, life is good. It's the day after Christmas and I'm writing these lines for you on my iPhone, chilling in bed. It's cold outside. Last night we just had another snowstorm and the power went out. My daughter, Margaux, is sitting next to me, reading. My wife, Joanne, is making a fire to keep us warm. Our dog Slinky is sleeping by my feet. We live in the San Bernardino Mountains, California, and today we're completely snowed in. All the trees are covered in snow. It's beautiful. No, it's majestic! Everything is so quiet.

Have you ever experienced the silence of the snow?

It's funny because in the forest there's normally a lot of echo. Sounds travel fast and bounce all around. But the snow has this capacity to absorb any sound, so everything feels different. The animals are hiding; the roads are closed. It's a perfect moment. A sacred moment.

And today finds me in a state of complete happiness. I've just turned fifty. I'm with the ones I love. I'm doing what I love (I'm a teacher), writing a new book—in bed, no less. What could be better? The new year is coming, which is also the start of a new decade. All is well, indeed.

Hold on . . .

You see, there's a twist.

This year, I went through a terrible health crisis. I was very close to dying.

Not good.

I'm going to skip the details because I don't want to scare you or gross you out, but I went to medical hell and back. And yes, after shaking hands with death (and her grabby, bony fingers), I've bounced back into life. To the great surprise of my doctors, after a surgery, I recovered amazingly well.

Boing! Just like that.

I mean, I may be oversimplifying here a little bit, but you get the idea: I'm alive.

And while I was in the hospital, not sure whether I would make it, I had to ask myself these two questions:

Question #1: Is there anything I wish I had done differently in my life?

For this one, because I've been practicing what I've been

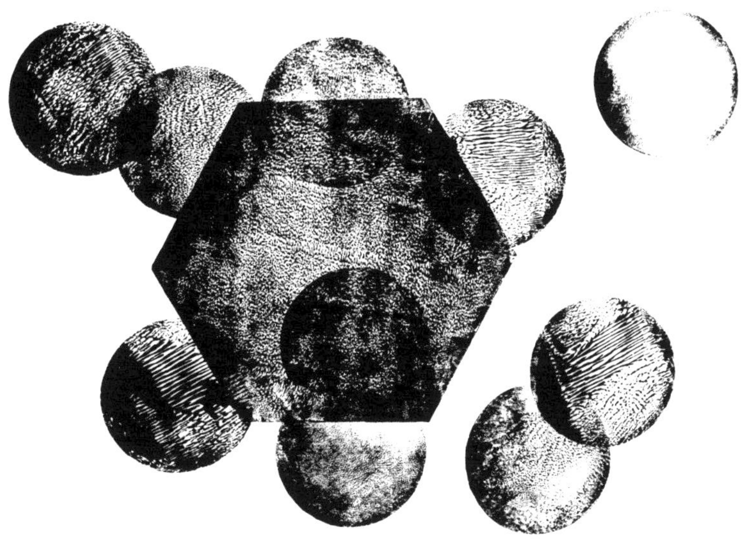

preaching all my adult life (creative living), the answer was no. Which was pretty cool (if you want to learn more about creative living, check out my book *You Are a Dream*).

Question #2: If I make it through this ordeal and get some extra time to live, what should I do with it?

And here, a couple of things popped up. I just wished for a few more simple experiences:

- Get a puppy for my daughter.
- Go camping with my family and spend quality time in nature together, away from everything.
- Eat a good carrot cake (that may sound silly to you, but I promise, when you're borderline dying at the hospital, carrot cake fantasies do occur).

Easy. Done, done, and *done!*

And then, one more thing . . .

- Write this one book about spirituality that I know I need to write.

All of a sudden, not so easy.

A warning

Life is short my creative, seeker friend. And, when you listen, life is calling you to do things that are outside of your comfort zone. *Always*. When this happens, you have to let go of your fears and jump into the unknown.

You have to bring your best.

And now, I'm starting this new journey with you. *Super Hyper Vibe!* is the spirituality book I've been meaning to write for two decades, but did not.

Why such a long time?

Well . . . From my perspective, spirituality is not what most people think it is. And when I say "most people," this includes spirituality teachers as well.

You see, what I'm about to share with you might be completely different from anything you've heard before.

The tone of this book is going to be different. In order to "touch the Real," I'm going to have to call a cat a cat. Point to the B.S. wherever I see it ("B.S." is our technical term for Boring Subterfuge, of course). Break some porcelain figurines. Use humor. Provoke you. All kinds of shenanigans.

This is going to be the ultimate wild ride, because we are going to talk about the Ultimate. Sometimes it will be joyful and inspiring; sometimes it will be hard. Very hard.

So if you're not ready, please close this book and run away.

If you're easily offended, please close this book and run away. If you consider yourself an expert on spirituality (which I'm sure you are because I am not), please close this book and run away.

The Real (with a big "R") is hard to find. The Ultimate (with a big "U") is elusive. What you will find (if you ever do find it) is not what you were looking for.

Sound confusing?

It is! And you know what to do: Close this book and run away.

The spiritual path is tricky. It's full of traps, monsters, evil magicians, and sorceresses—that's right! Spirituality is about finding light, but for many it actually becomes a dead end in the darkness. You think I'm kidding? I'm not.

The danger is real.

What?! You've never heard that spirituality can be dangerous? Close this book and run away. I'm being really serious here.

I'm warning you one last time! Close this book and run away!

You're still here?

HELLO, FRIEND!
G
6
9

Okay.

Maybe you're sensing that this book's curious title might just hide the thing you've been looking for?

Let's find out . . .

Let's start walking together. Come along. We have many things to explore.

In this book, I want to talk with you about the greatest gift you've ever received: your life. I also want to show you a path that will nurture your life in a way that's filled with meaning, love, growth, creativity, connection, and beauty. A path where you can actually win the spiritual game of your life by reconciling opposites. A path where you can let your spirit shine, here and now. A path where you will be vibing the *Super Hyper Vibe!*

This book is divided into four parts.

In Part 1, **Into the World**, we're going to find your entry point onto the spiritual path, by looking at what's happening in your life right now. We're also going to take a look at a couple of obstacles you need to tackle before you begin your journey.

In Part 2, **Reunion Path**, I will be sharing principles and directions to guide you and move you from spiritual fragmentation into wholeness. This will be the map to help you reconcile opposites that your Soul has been waiting for.

In Part 3, **Workshop**, I will guide and challenge you through a seven-day process to discover the reality of the Soul through

Reunion practices and exercises.

In Part 4, **Game Changers**, we are going to discover how to play the game of your life by changing it.

Are you interested?
Are you excited?
Are you ready?

Okay, then let's begin.
Because guess what?

I'm interested.
I'm excited.
And I'm ready too!

Let's go!

With love,
Guillaume Wolf "Prof. G"

Lake Arrowhead, California, December 26,
from the blessed moment of the here and the now

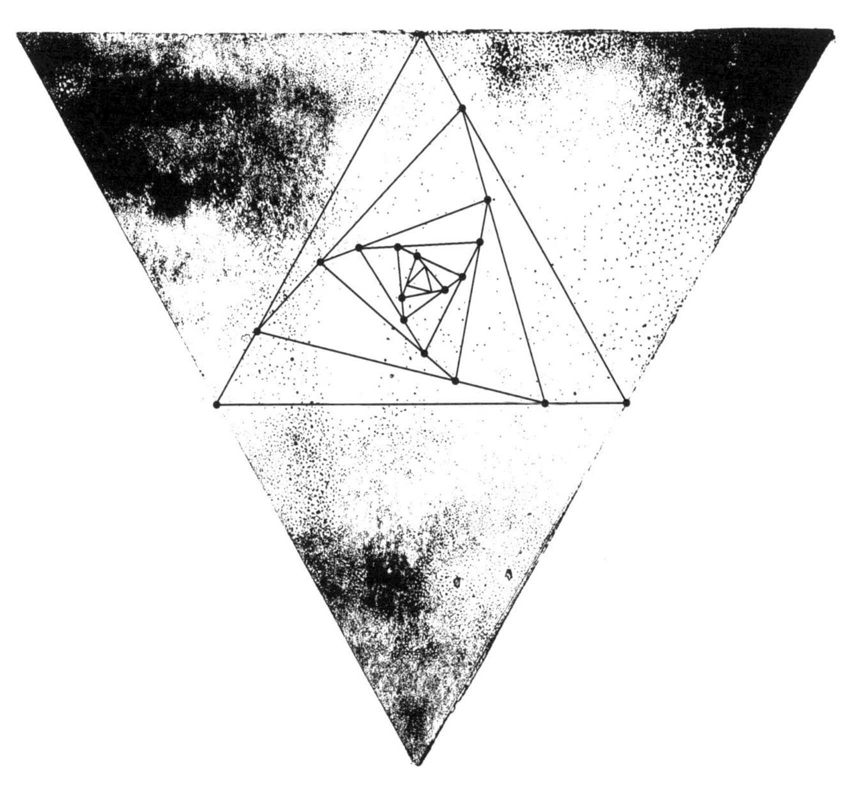

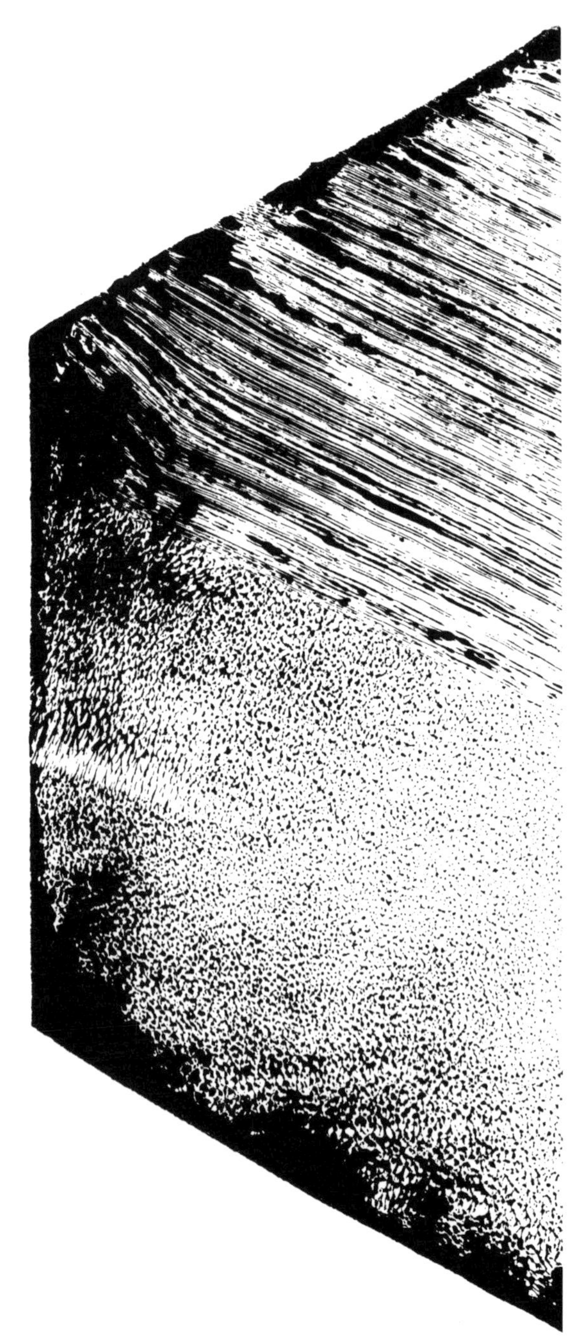

PART 1

INTO THE WORLD

In this introduction, I want to talk about the prep work you need to do before you can walk on the spiritual path, and I'll share with you what led me to it. I'm also going to reveal some of the dangers that might be lurking there (because there are many). This part of the book is a little bit like cleaning your house before receiving your guests for a little stay over—it's a must. Please read it very carefully.

Oh yes, I forgot . . . This is also the part where I'm going to pour water on sand castles, throw rocks at conventions, kick doors open, start some fires, and challenge the heck out of you. So hang tight!

Hello, how are you?
So you're still here, reading this book. Great. Now I'm going to ask you this:

Why?

What prompted you to pick up this book?

Look, the title is weird. *Super Hyper Vibe!* is enigmatic at best.

It might be just hype, okay?

Who is this "Prof. G" character anyway? Do you know this guy? Prof. G? Come on!

Seriously, why are you reading this?

Well, let me guess.

You are a Soul Being living on this planet called Earth. You've landed here, out of nowhere. Now, you're now-here (you can read that twice). Brutal landing? Yes. Did you arrive in a perfect reality, where you were loved unconditionally and taught to be self-reliant, creative, and strong? Probably not. Did you avoid being hurt? Nope. How bad has it been for you?

Probably really bad.
Life can be brutal, I know.

Or maybe you come from a completely different perspective. Maybe you're still very young, or you've been living your life sheltered, even overprotected. Your life may have been uneventful; but in many ways, even if on the surface everything looks fine, it feels like you're surrounded by a gray haze. You wonder, "Is that all there is?"

And now you're looking for something.

Somehow, somewhere, something has pushed you beyond the edge of your reality. A tiny whack on your head has forced you to open your eyes and wake up—even for an instant. You may have seen (or sensed) that there's much more to the picture than what you've been told at home, at school, at work, or at

church. Maybe, through pain, injustice, or simply boredom, you've developed a desire to taste the transcendent. Maybe you're looking for this ultimate, infinite Love (with a big "L") that mystics have been talking about for centuries. The Love that nurtures the Soul. Or maybe you've experienced the random sighting of simple beauty (you never know with these things), a fleeting moment of deep peace that's almost impossible to describe. Like watching a shooting star. So beautiful. So fast.

You, my friend, are a seeker.

I know this isn't the easiest place to be in. Sometimes it feels terribly lonely. And very few people (if any) know this about you, because, amazingly, you've also found the courage to move forward and build a life for yourself. And that's great. "You're so great," many of your friends might even say to you, once in a while. Yes, on the outside, you look okay. You act okay. But inside something is missing. They don't know how thirsty you are for that spiritual glimpse. That droplet of light that can bring meaning to the senselessness you've experienced before, and that you still see everywhere when you look around.

Yes, you are a seeker, and it's both a blessing and a curse.

If this is you, I'd like to welcome you as you are today, in all your humanity. I'm writing this book for you.

And now, as a welcome gift (yes, it's a thing here), I'd like to share some good news with you. These are the opening words to the poem "The Quest" by the Sufi mystic Rumi. Here's what he says: "Even if you're not equipped, keep searching. Equipment is not necessary on the way to the Lord."

Listen, if right now you're full of self-doubt, if you feel you lack knowledge, courage, wisdom, or resolve, please remember the words of Rumi: You don't need any equipment. Bring your heart. Bring your truth. Your soul is good to go to enter the spiritual game of your own life.

Again, come as you are. Search with me. Let's go together and look for the Real. It's such an honor to be talking with you, in all your glorious, perfect imperfection. I see you, all of you, my creative, seeker friend. And I feel blessed that we're spending this time together.

Get total clarity before you start

Now I'd like to share something else with you, and it's a bit trickier. I know that this is going to sound weird, but here it is:

> Your lock is your doorway.

Whatever trouble you may have in your life today, you can imagine it as a lock; a lock with a missing key, something you need to crack open. But look again. This lock, no matter how horrible, boring, or painful it might be, is also your doorway! It's your entry point into the spiritual path. Without it, you would not be a seeker to begin with.

This is one of these paradoxes of spiritual life. And it's the first one you need to be aware of, right now. Whatever brought you on the path is also what's propelling you to move forward in the search for discovery and knowledge. Without it, there would be no movement and you would still be in a state of semi-sleep or apathy.

Unlike simple mathematics, spiritual life is full of strange paradoxes like this one. The spiritual path leads to the land of paradoxes that also happens to be the domain of the Soul. It's impenetrable to the mind. You can enter it only with your heart (and with a lot of love).

So whatever you've been dealt (or are currently dealing with), know that it can act as a spark to remember that you are a Soul. I mean it. But watch out—even when talking about it, we need to tread very carefully. With real compassion.

It's important for you to see the large picture. Your life is a complex, whole living system. A system so complex, in fact, that you can forget about ever figuring it out with your mind alone. There's a Zen proverb that suggests this idea artfully: "The snow falls, each flake in its appropriate place."

Trying to use your intellect to search for ultimate meaning always leads to a dead end. Your mind cannot grasp the infinite complexity of your own life, and if you ask it to do so, it will always return empty-handed. This explains why philosophy and science (which are mind-based) can't help us when it comes to our Soul journey. In the search for ultimate meaning, the mind always comes back, arrogantly, with the answer: "Life has no meaning." Is this true, though? Or does it simply reflect the mind's own limitations?

Hear this: Using only your mind in an attempt to get an answer for your Soul is the silliest thing you can do. You can't grasp or control your life with mind power. It simply doesn't work. But what you can do is *connect* with your life through presence. That's an important distinction and a key to total spiritual transformation.

And how can you create this connection with your life? First, you need to stop hiding (hiding is an attempt at controlling) and start telling the truth about yourself. You must find the courage to look where you don't want to look. And that's hard. It takes a lot of heart to go to the haunted place of your memory. I call this place "the horribleness." No one wants to go there, for a reason. It takes real courage.

And here, because I have nothing to hide in our conversation, I'm going to go first, and share my horribleness with you. This is where I'm coming from.

My horribleness

I was born in Dakar, Senegal, a wonderful country on the West Coast of Africa. There my very French parents were busy living the seventies hedonistic lifestyle and decided to pass me along to a local male nanny named Mamadou. Which meant that for the first years of my life, I was raised by an African man. This slightly different early life left my senses attuned to vibrant lights and colors, rhythms. Human warmth. Simple beauty.

Then, eventually, we all had to go back to France. On our last day in Dakar, Mamadou broke down and cried out that, without him, I wouldn't survive—which, it turned out, almost became a prophecy.

As I was growing up in Paris, my mother became a full-blown alcoholic. My absentee, enabling father supported her in her addiction. And so, with this setup—like a cold, automated system—before the age of ten I had experienced psychological violence, physical violence, and sexual violence. It turned out that the most dangerous place for a small child was not Africa; it was France.

This is what I've started my life with, the trifecta of pain. My horribleness.

In her worst drunken daze, my mom used to beat me with a horsewhip. "Why a horsewhip?" you may ask. She clarified this years later with cold logic: "I had hurt my hand after beating your brothers so many times that I needed something to avoid hurting myself again."

When I was around eight, I was sexually molested by a doctor. During a consultation, he probably sniffed the wine on my mom and found a way to get rid of her. And, later on, I was completely ignored when I found the courage to talk about it with my parents. Denial was their go-to strategy for everything. Including this. They simply would not hear what I was saying (which is, I've since discovered, a common pattern in cases of sexual abuse). They even insisted that I keep seeing this doctor—but I said no. Learning to say no is good. In this instance, it was a life-saving move.

I was raised Catholic, baptized, confirmed, and all, but in Catholic school I had to deal with anti-Semitic slurs and physical attacks because I had the wrong last name. This definitely opened my eyes about the infinite stupidity of racism and bigotry, and how it's passed on from one generation to the next. Being called "a dirty Jew" without actually being Jewish myself was an experience straight out of a Kafka novel that forced me to think deeper about reality. But worry not, my friend—this also taught me how to defend myself and stand my own ground.

Now, I could share more, but this book isn't about me, it's about you.

So let's talk about you.

This horribleness that you might be dealing with (past or present), no matter how bad it is, always hides the possibility of a deeper mystery.

This is very important: It can really be an entry point, if you decide to make it so. For me, this brutal start opened the door for a lifelong spiritual search that taught me about healing, creativity, compassion, strength, and love. And later in life, to my great surprise, it also connected me with the higher reality of the Soul—a gift I never expected to receive.

Here, I've shared with you my personal trifecta of pain and how it prompted my journey. Being able to state your horribleness (whatever it might be) is also the first step into awareness and healing. Before you can safely explore spirituality (the Soul), you need to start at the psychological level (the mind). It's very important prep work because it ignites the awakening of the Soul. There's no shortcut for it.

In direct opposition, there's denial (self-lying). Denial is pure spiritual poison—it's the surest way to numb and bury your Soul. Remember, self-lying is spiritual self-dying. Don't do it.

So, for example, if you're depressed all the time and you don't know why, or if you're plagued with anxiety for no (apparent) reason, remember that these are only symptoms. You don't need a secret mantra, or a "course in manifestation" to change your life. It's not gonna help. First, you need to stop and take a very long look at your biography and identify the horribleness you've been dealt. Call it what it is. And if you need to spend some time with a healing professional or a fellow seeker to talk about your stuff, *go for it*. You can also do it through journaling. Let it out! Take a deep breath. Uncover what is hidden. Put some light onto it. Say what you need to say, and release it. It might be very painful at first, but it will help you gain back your strength.

This is very powerful because by doing a clear inventory of your past first, you will find clarity and compassion for yourself. (Here's some good advice, by the way: Stop being so hard on yourself!) And then you can slowly uncover the fact that you are not your biography (you don't need to identify with it—it is what it is, and that's all).

Instead, you might uncover that this thing you call "you" is an ongoing process of growth and transformation (we'll talk more about this later). And you might even discover that you are a Soul. Not as an idea, but as a reality to be experienced, day by day. That's pretty amazing.

This should be your first move before you start on your spiritual path. And here I recommend that you do it with intent. Decide to look. Look. Identify what is not okay. Have complete clarity. This is your first step. I know it's not fun and you might not want to do it, but the work we're doing here together will guide you to become a *conqueror* of life, not just a survivor. And while these two words might echo one another, they are completely different.

Think about it.

Avoid this one mistake.
Watch out: Looking at your horribleness straight in the eyes is the first step, but it isn't enough. One of the (many) traps of

spiritual life is to believe that this first step is all you need to accomplish. This belief follows a sequence that goes more or less like this:

- You've suffered.
- You've identified the suffering.
- You've survived it.
- You've done a little bit of healing work.
- In the process, you've developed a high sensitivity, some insight about life and yourself.
- Therefore you start believing you will be magically rewarded by life (you might even secretly think you're special—after all, you've survived, didn't you?), because if not, it would mean that life is meaningless.
- And because life can't be meaningless (after all your suffering), then you must be special in some way and entitled to unique rewards.

Don't fall for this. This is faulty logic. I've seen this pattern over and over with many holistic healers, yoga teachers, creatives, and spiritual seekers. It's very common because it happens automatically. This is an extremely dangerous delusion. A superb self-created trap. You can call it magical thinking, and it leads to narcissism. And it's bad.

Why?

Because that's not how life works. You can be beaten up a million times by life and you may have survived the ordeal. And it's awesome that you've passed through it—I really mean it. But that doesn't make you special in any shape or form. Thinking you're special is your ego mind (or Persona) acting out. Believe it for one second and your Soul journey is over.

You will disconnect from the spiritual game of your life.

That's not what you want!

Your Soul is here to shine! Remember, "you," as a person, are not "special"; however, you are a Soul having a very special human experience. We all do.

Why is this experience so special?

To begin with, it is limited in time. And you have the possibility to co-create how it's going to unfold. Isn't that amazing enough? No? How about this: To reveal its magic and deep beauty, Life (with a big "L") is waiting for you to show your true colors and play full on! Life wants you to open your eyes. Right now, Life is inviting your Soul to play the spiritual game of your life. Can't you hear her calling your name?

Listen!
She's doing it now!
Come on! *Listen!*

Let's dump all the gurus!

Note: Because I'm not a fan of gurus, I initially thought I would unleash hell and drop massive F-bombs all over this chapter. But eventually I realized that it wouldn't make for very interesting wordsmithing. So instead, I've decided to explore something new by researching vintage English insults for our shared entertainment. Let's see how many you can spot below!

Okay, first I have a confession to make: As an author, I've always wanted to write, "Let's dump all the gurus!" in a book about spirituality. Why? Because it needs to be said. And I mean it.

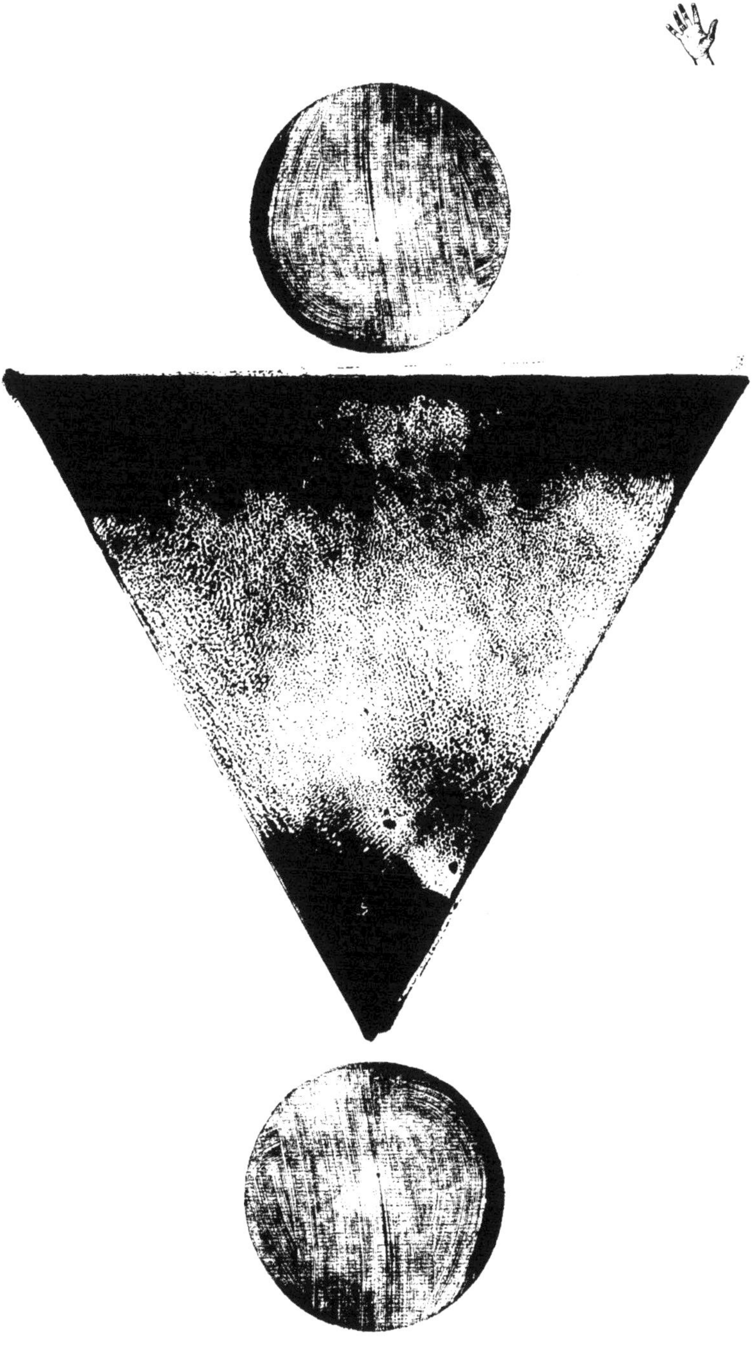

When you start your spiritual journey, it's a little bit like arriving in a foreign land without having a map. Maybe you'll begin by exploring the aisles of a spiritual bookstore, maybe you'll go to a retreat, or maybe a friend will share some recommendations with you. The truth is, you have *no idea* where you're going. Not only that, you're also looking for something without exactly knowing what this "thing" is. So you start exploring randomly, hoping to eventually discover what you're looking for. It turns out that this strategy leaves you with more questions than answers. You might find yourself a little bit lost and confused. And later, as you move forward, you'll discover that there are many signs pointing in the direction of a guru. By that time, you'll be tired of searching, and you'll ask yourself: "Is this benevolent-looking guru the way to liberation?"

Good question. But first, what is a guru exactly?

On a surface level, the translation of guru is "teacher." But is it accurate?

A teacher is a normal human being, someone who shares knowledge with his/her students so they can grow by developing skills that will make them successful in their lives.

Here's the catch: A guru is *nothing* like a teacher.

A guru is someone who claims to have reached (and to be the embodiment of) psychological, intellectual, and spiritual perfection. Not only that, the guru also claims that he/she is the only way to God/Enlightenment/Nirvana/Paradise. With this statement, the guru is binding you, *not* liberating you. If you follow the guru, you will find that there is pressure to give up your critical thinking as you will be told, over and over, to

"surrender to the guru." You can imagine the guru standing between you and the Great Infinite, holding a stop sign.

Now, should you trust your Soul with this fustilarian?

Heck, no! Let me go over this with you quickly.

The game gurus play is complete B.S., because no one can ever claim perfection. Perfection cannot exist in this reality. Perfection, for a human, would mean reaching an ultimate, finite state of being. A static form. But life itself can only exist as a process of growth and evolution. Life can't be static, because it always changes. Life is ongoing, infinite transformation. You and every other human being on this planet are growing and evolving—no exceptions. And that's wonderful, really. Therefore, anyone claiming to have attained perfection is a lickspittle of the lowest order with zero understanding of life, both physically and spiritually. Any claim of perfection is, by definition, void. Perfection in any shape or form is anti-life itself.

In addition, the other claim, that the guru is "your only connection with the divine," is completely bogus. It's the greatest lie of all. Life wants *YOU* to create and nourish that connection. It might be hard, but it's your job! That's why you're here on this plane of existence!

Here let me do a quick analogy with dating: Imagine you want to date someone and create a meaningful connection with this person. And then, all of a sudden, a "love guru" shows up at your doorstep and claims to be the only one who can help you realize this connection (thanks to a special mystical love power of sorts). Then the guru adds: "Without me, you will never succeed in finding love."

Would you believe this charlatan? Of course not.

See? That was fast.

Know that the goal of the guru is to always try to infantilize you by asserting superiority over you. This is called the guru game. It's a toxic power play that only benefits the guru. The more you hang out with a guru, the more he/she will deplete your Soul power.

This is not news, by the way. In his spectacular 1929 speech dissolving the Order of the Star, the spiritual teacher (and my personal hero) Jiddu Krishnamurti revealed the con. This is an incredible moment in history, because in early childhood Krishnamurti had been adopted, and later trained, by a spiritual organization to become *THE* ultimate guru. Turns out, he wanted none of it. Here's what he said on that day, in front of his three thousand followers.

"I have decided, as I happen to be the Head of the Order, to dissolve it." Later, he added, "The moment you follow someone, you cease to follow Truth."

Boom! This is possibly the biggest, and boldest spiritual microphone drop the world has ever seen. And that's why Krishnamurti—who was a real teacher, and not a guru—is one of my favorite authors.

He told the truth as he saw it. And that's a precious gift.

But one powerful truth is not enough to change the world. And

just as with bedbugs in New York hotels, today we are facing an ever-growing guru infestation problem.

Offline or online, countless gurus are promoting insane ideas to attract and entrap their followers (because the nuttier the claim, the better). For example, some cullions are claiming to be so spiritual that they can sustain their lives without food or water, simply by breathing. Another mumblecrust I know claims to be the last heir to some ancient forgotten tradition he has invented. And, because these days we're completely spinning out of control, you can even find swarms of scobberlotchers explaining to whoever wants to hear them that they are multidimensional beings, extraterrestrials, or even avatars (sometimes, all of the above, because, why not?). It's hard to keep track. Look: There's a guy in Australia who claims to be Jesus. But wait! Look over there! There's another guy, in Russia, who claims to be Jesus as well!

Ten years ago, at a yoga retreat, I personally met a smellfungus who was teaching a workshop, and completely out of nowhere, he told us he was Lord Shiva himself (one of the main deities of Hinduism). *Seriously*.

Here's the beginning of our encounter:

> Him: Hello, everyone, I am Maha Shiva [meaning "the Great Shiva" in Sanskrit].
>
> Me [raising my hand]: Should we call you Great Shiva? Shiva? Or Mister Shiva?
>
> Him [frowning]: Shiva is fine.

> Me: When you go to Starbucks, and they ask your name, do you say "John" or "Maha Shiva"?

As you can imagine, it went downhill from there. I just pushed a tiny little bit and within five minutes the entire muntz-watcher facade collapsed. It was kind of funny. The great, exalted one lost his cool and threw a temper tantrum.

Gurus (and wannabe gurus) have zero sense of humor when it comes to their claims to perfection. And this rigid encrustation reveals their B.S. (Boring Subterfuge) to begin with. Because the nature of the guru-devotee relationship is authoritarian, the guru needs to keep projecting this idea of perfection at all costs. If there's one crack, the whole illusion collapses. Authoritarian structures demand blind respect in order to control.

Later in this book, we'll talk about spiritual liberation and how there are many sociocultural systems in place to keep us from ever attaining it. If you truly care about your spiritual life, you seriously need to wake up to the fact that the guru game is designed to keep you bound to the guru, *not* to help you attain liberation. Please realize this: You don't need a guru simply because (if you pay attention) Life *is* your guru!

I know this point of view will stir controversy (I see you, my dear Yoga friends), but what I'm talking about has been widely documented. And if you're shocked, please start reading *The Guru Papers: Masks of Authoritarian Power* (1993) by Joel Kramer to dig deeper. You can also watch the amazing documentary *Wild Wild Country* (2018) on Netflix.

You don't need a spiritual middleman to help you build a relationship with the Infinite. Why? Because that relationship is already there. You are living it now! *You* are it!

Spirituality versus Religion

When you study religions, you can always find beauty in the original voice of the prophet/messiah. And that's amazing.

But years later, after the prophet is long gone, a church is created by people of a different kind. And sadly, we sometimes move from spiritual well-being to spiritual exploitation. For example, do a simple Web search on "abuse in the Catholic Church" and you'll find countless horrific stories. Next, do another search on "sexual abuse in Buddhism" and you'll find more horror stories. It never ends. It's not about one specific faith; it's about authoritarian power and exploitation.

This is beyond comprehension.

When this happens, two crimes are being committed, in my opinion. First, there's the actual physical crime. Second, there's the spiritual crime of using religion as a mask for power and abuse that ends up making people run away from their church/temple, and therefore simultaneously robbing from them the experience of the divine. This is the darkest thing you can imagine. Pure evil.

Religion is also a place for rules that have more to do with social control and judgment than spiritual well-being. This failure to provide a real, meaningful spiritual experience is also the reason why we see that mainstream religions are in deep decline worldwide. This goes even deeper. Many seekers who have been scarred by their experiences with religion can't even use the word "God" anymore. They have replaced it with "the Creator," "the Infinite," etc. So here, to break the spell, I will occasionally use the word "God" in this book. Why? Just because. God is Love (with a big "L"). It shouldn't be a scary word for anyone. We're not here to live in fear.

Agreed?

Now, watch out! Do you hear pleasant chimes? Do you smell delightful incense? Look this way! On the other side of the road, here comes spirituality with its big smile.

Spirituality, on the other hand, can be defined as a practice (individual or collective) where the only goal is to liberate and nurture the Soul. It can take multiple shapes and forms. Spirituality is cross-cultural in nature because what counts is the direct experience itself, not the rules. It's the path of the mystic, not of the follower. To put it simply, it's awesome.

But this freedom can also rapidly become a problem. Without any structure, the vaporized nature of spirituality can be extremely shallow.

California is a fantastic place to experience this spiritual shallowness combined with spiritual materialism (it's often a two-for-one deal). The general attitude that suggests "My crystal is bigger than yours, therefore my spirituality is superior to yours" is something that I've experienced multiple times in the Los Angeles "spiritual" community. Status plays a big part in these circles. This is really weird to me.

But there's more . . .

Because modern spirituality is so post-postmodern, absolutely anything goes. Anything. There are no rules, remember? To the point of complete absurdity. Let me share an example.

I recall a conversation I had in L.A. with a well-established New Age healer who told me she'd had a special vision of "Count Saint-Germaine" (that's not how you spell his name) who apparently had shown her all the secret, magical places in Paris (which was convenient, because this lady had never actually visited the place). In the New Age world, Saint-Germain (no "e" at the end) is believed to be an immortal being.

Okay. At that point, my ears were bleeding a tiny little bit, but it's fine to be confused about the spelling of foreign names—we're all human. But then she wrote a blog post about it, again misspelling his name. When I very, very gently (I promise) pointed out to her that the venerable count's name was Saint-Germain (not Saint-Germaine), she stayed completely poker-faced and told me that *HE* had told her (in her vision) that was how his name should be spelled! Well, that was news to me, someone who actually grew up in Paris, France, in a district called Saint-Germain-des-Prés (where you'll find Paris's oldest church). You see, it becomes really silly when you tell the locals of a place that you know nothing about how to spell words from their own language.

The problem with a no-judgment-anything-goes-attitude that's left completely unchecked is that in the very beginning it might look caring and open—because, remember, a lot of folks who go into spirituality have run away from the judgmental hammer of traditional religions and crave this freedom. But then, really quickly, you end up dwelling in complete nonsense. It's lazy. Worst of all, it's spiritually corrupt.

Of course, this wasn't just one isolated incident. Let me recall my formative years, meeting with the most celebrated spiritual teachers. Here's what happened: Fake. Fake. Fake. And . . .

Wait for it . . . (Oops, never mind.) *Fake!*

Isn't it interesting to discover so much fakeness when your goal is to find the Real?

To put it this way, if today you're a serious seeker standing at the crossroad between religion and spirituality, you might find yourself stuck in a spiritual double bind: You're damned if you do. You're damned if you don't.

So what do you do?

Understanding Gnosis

When we approach things of a spiritual nature, we're culturally conditioned to think about religion. But, as I've already mentioned, religion comes years after the original voice of a prophet, and it rarely has much in common with it. A prophet is a prophet because he/she has a direct experience of, and a relationship with, God/the Infinite. This direct experience of the divine is called *gnosis* in ancient Greek. It's the knowledge of spiritual mysteries. But gnosis is far more than intellectual knowledge—it's Soul knowledge. Like love, it's not something that you can explain intellectually; it's something you have to experience. When you are a spiritual seeker, your goal is gnosis.

Where can you find gnosis?

(Watch out my creative, seeker friend—I might be a spiritual trickster, and this might be a trick question.)

Do you need to travel to a specific place?
An ancient temple in Egypt? A beautiful church in Europe?

Or perhaps a secret spiritual hot spot on a remote mountain in India?

Or:

Could you find gnosis waiting at the checkout line in your local grocery store? In your interaction with a homeless person? Changing a tire on your car? Catching a spider? Washing the dishes? When you're sick? Cutting your fingernails? Hiking? Hugging? Having sex?

Where is it?

Could gnosis be nowhere and everywhere at the same time? This is a very good question.

The problem with "ancient" traditions

One final obstacle I want to share with you is the fallacy of tradition. Note: Before I go there, just know that if you happen to follow a tradition and you're happy with it, that's wonderful. Stick with it. Grow into it.

Let's imagine you've done all the prep work I mentioned before, and you'd like to commit to one spiritual practice. Great. Now which aisle should you be looking for in the spiritual supermarket? As a reasonable person, you'll be tempted to explore something in the "ancient tradition" section (it's aisle 7, by the way, next to the cookies). After all, what could be more reassuring than choosing a path that has been practiced for hundreds—no, even better—thousands of years! And as a bonus, some old traditions even allow you to dress up in exotic costumes, which is always a plus if you want to instantly feel spiritually superior.

If it's old, it must be real, right?

Well, maybe. Let's find out.

Tradition implies linear time. But from the mystic's perspective, there's a big problem: *Absolutely nothing exists outside of the present moment*. The present moment is a single point that encompasses everything. It's not linear. You're always in the present. If you're studying an ancient book, you're doing it, right here, right now. Your experience of it is located in the present moment.

As an example, if today you were to travel to China to study Daoism (which boasts a history of over 2,500 years), well . . . you would be doing it now, in this very present moment. Don't delude yourself. Your shifu ("master," 师傅), even if he/she has a superb silvery beard and a matching long robe, is a modern dude/dudette, just like you (And yes, a Daoist master dudette can have a superb silvery beard, too). Because you are in the present, you are therefore studying a completely modern version of Daoism. Period.

Here, a spiritual expert might come into our conversation in an attempt to debunk this statement by saying that it's the practice that has been unchanged for thousands of years, and this is where the value is. In fact, many spiritual groups insist on their "lineage" to boost their credibility. But, again, if that were truly the case, we would talk about a crystallized, finite practice that would exist outside of time. This would be a dead practice. Again, anything that doesn't grow and evolve with life in the here and now is dead. It's true for people, trees, relationships, communities, languages, and also spiritual practices. Again, nothing exists outside of the present moment. Absolutely nothing.

Tradition is attractive but in and of itself it is yet another spiritual trap. It doesn't mean anything on its own. However, please don't get me wrong, ancient traditions contain infinite treasures of wisdom (I love them deeply), when, and only when, this wisdom is infused and rejuvenated by the spark of the present moment. I'm sharing this with you because our pesky gurus love to use tradition as a way to assert their superiority (and that's why there are so many beards, hats, and special outfits in the guru world: For them, it's important to look the part by playing the "ancient tradition" card). It captures the imagination. And capturing the imagination is the first goal of the actor who's playing a part.

Hmmm . . .

A spiritual truth that reveals the transcendent in life is not transferable over time, like a house deed. In reality, it's more like an ocean wave. It's always there, coming and going, forever evolving, right in front of you. You can't contain it. But if you have good balance, and if you pay attention to the now, you can connect with it. How? Grab a board and try surfing it. See what happens.

Sound like fun to you?

Maybe it's because it is.

Now what?

As a younger seeker, I was profoundly disgusted (there's no other way to say it) by what I uncovered in the spiritual community at large. And yes, I did look really broadly: Eastern philosophies, Western philosophies, traditional, nontraditional, old religions, new religions, New Age. Even the occult (for kicks).

Every time, I found the same patterns everywhere I looked: deeply flawed teachers, playing a role. The exploitative, predatory nature of the guru game. Shallowness. Never-ending spiritual drama. Petty fights about the local pecking order. Greed. Gross display of excessive wealth. Lust for status and fame. Stories of abuse.

Now that I'm much older, I'm completely at peace with this state of affairs. There are deeper reasons why things are the way they are, and we will talk about them later in the book.

But back then, seeing so much fakeness, I did what seemed to be the most sensible thing at the time: I completely turned my back on this "spiritual world." I closed down this chapter in my life (the first book I had ever written was actually a spirituality book) and moved on. I set my spiritual practice to "private mode," deepening it for the next two decades, happily thinking I would never have to talk publicly about spirituality again.

Surprisingly, this was the correct move as it created the freedom (time and space) to explore and uncover what I was actually really looking for. So what had at first seemed a massive disappointment turned out to be the greatest gift of all.

And then, out of nowhere, my brief encounter with the grim reaper gave me the push to write this book and to share with you what I've discovered during these twenty years of reflection.

Life is kinda funny like that.

This is so important!
Why am I taking the time to share all this with you?

My goal in writing this book is to offer you something of value. Something transformative. And when I'm bringing my super flashlight to shine some light in a field that's cluttered with a lot of deceit, outmoded ideas and practices, know that there's a reason behind it.

In doing so, I'm actually participating in an ancient tradition that the Greeks called *parrhesia* (παρρησία), which means "bold speech," or "frankness." In today's slang we would call *parrhesia* "dropping some truth bombs."

In Athenian democracy, *parrhesia* was a core duty of the Greek citizen: speaking the truth, even if the population was not ready for it. Today, *parrhesia* is almost completely gone from modern society. But let me ask you this: How can you honestly talk about spirituality and look for the Real without daring to speak your own truth?

I'm fully aware that I might offend some people in the process. I'm also clear that the ideas I'm bringing forward are not for everyone (for example, if you love your guru, keep at it). But regardless, I feel moved to express myself because, to me, spirituality isn't a popularity contest. In my heart of hearts, I know that this is a very serious conversation.

I believe that we are at a turning point in history where spirituality needs to be rejuvenated with something new. I also believe that we need to upgrade our spiritual culture with a radically different approach. And there's a certain sense of urgency here. The clock is ticking.

Yet know this: I'm not a guru. I don't have special powers. I'm a seeker of truth, just like you. I'm both a teacher and a student, and I'm learning new things every day (what a gift this is!). I simply have a perspective to share and I sincerely hope that it can make a difference in your life as it did in mine.

In this conversation, we are working together to explore and celebrate Life and the Soul. The keyword here is the word *"together."*

This is so important!

You see, we live in divisive times that are characterized by fear: fear of the future, fear of the unknown, fear of "the other," fear of expressing oneself. This is the great age of separation, the age of bunkerization where every individual constructs and lives in a separate little bubble. And it's completely absurd.

Today, as conscious human beings, it's time for us to wake up and rise up collectively to the challenge of our generation: We urgently need to come together and bring unity back into our lives. This will not come from fundamentalist spiritual or political ideologies (which always bring more division); nor will it come from following gurus. I believe we need to try something new: doing the work together by going deep inside our hearts to experience the reality of the Soul (and its incredible power), so we can act from that perspective.

You and I are both Soul Beings sharing the same journey on our beautiful planet Earth. We are sons and daughters of the Infinite. We all come from the great unknown and we shall return to it. Our journey starts in separateness and unawareness, and as we wake up, it moves toward Unity.

This is such a unique adventure!

The journey begins with:
"I am alone."
Then it continues with a lovely:
"We are together."
And later, when it clicks, it explodes into a transcendent sound that travels through all the levels of existence, a roar that says:
"I AM!"

We are one: Diversity in Unity, Unity in Diversity.

So, if I have the pleasure of meeting you in the future, I hope you will recognize our Soul kinship so we can celebrate together the gift of the present moment, as one.

Together, we can create something new. We can infuse our reality with courage and love. And whenever we get blinded by hate, apathy, and cynicism, we can take a stand by revealing hope, creativity, and possibilities.

I simply call this practice Reunion. It's a movement that takes us from fragmentation into spiritual wholeness—not as a form of escapism, but as an engaged way of being in the world that allows us to grow and evolve, to create and experience freedom and love.

Now, shall we begin this journey together?

You are a Soul Being
living on this planet called Earth.
You've landed here, out of nowhere.
Now, you're now-here.

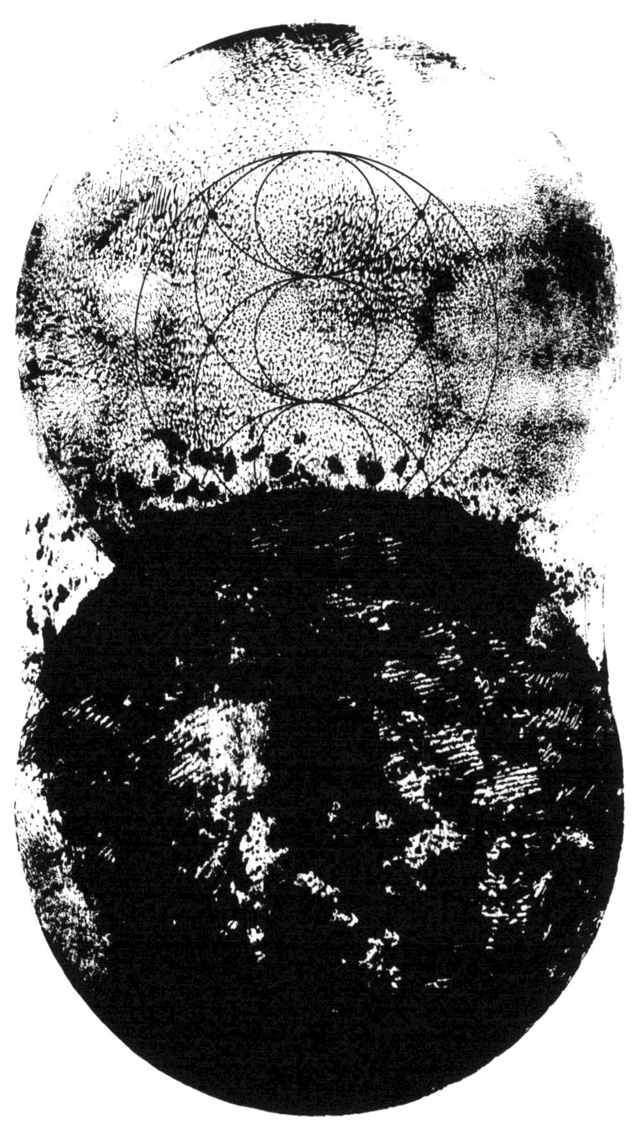

Your life is a complex, whole living system.
A system so complex, in fact, that you can forget about ever figuring it out with your mind alone.

But what you can do is *connect* with your life through presence.

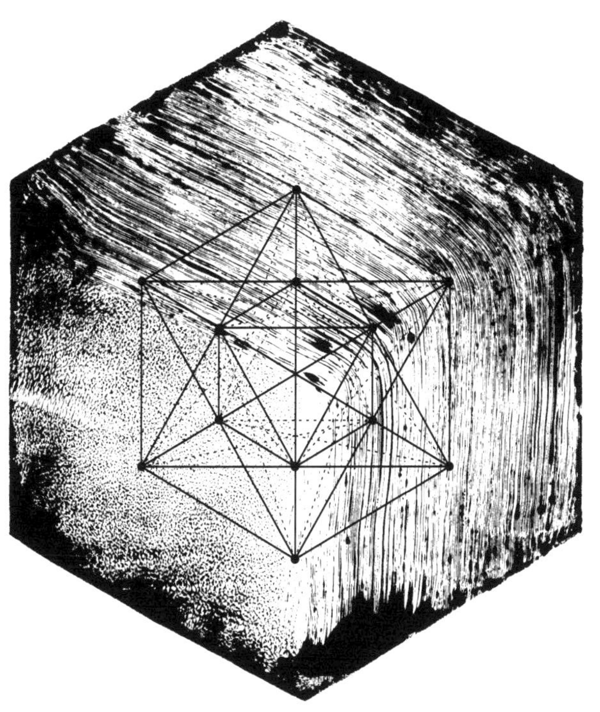

To reveal its magic and deep beauty, Life is waiting for you to show your true colors and play full on!

Life wants you to open your eyes.

Right now, Life is inviting your Soul
to play the spiritual game of your life.
Can't you hear her calling your name?

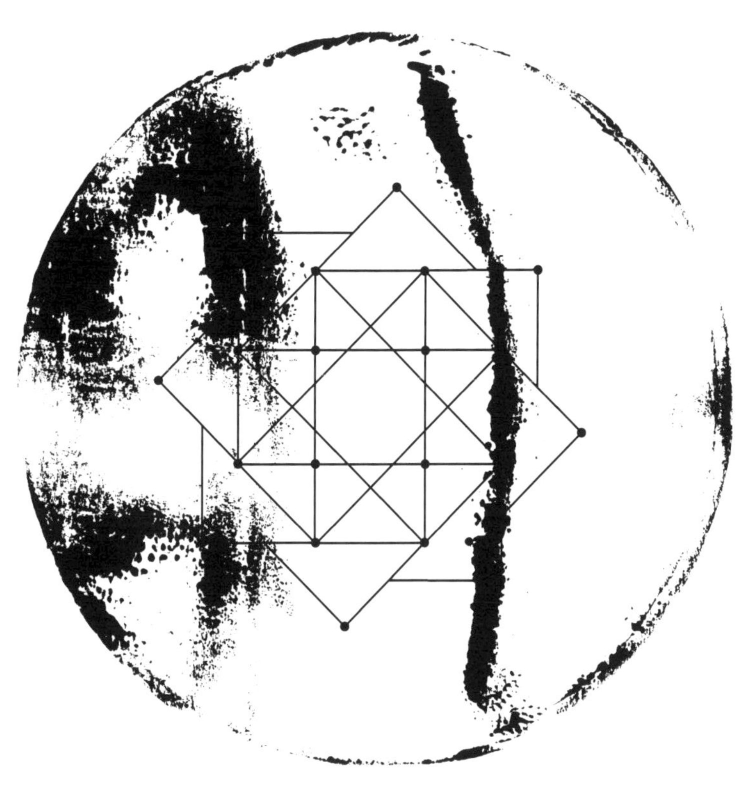

We are sons and daughters of the Infinite.
We all come from the great unknown
and we shall return to it.
Our journey starts in separateness
and unawareness, and as we wake up,
it moves toward Unity.

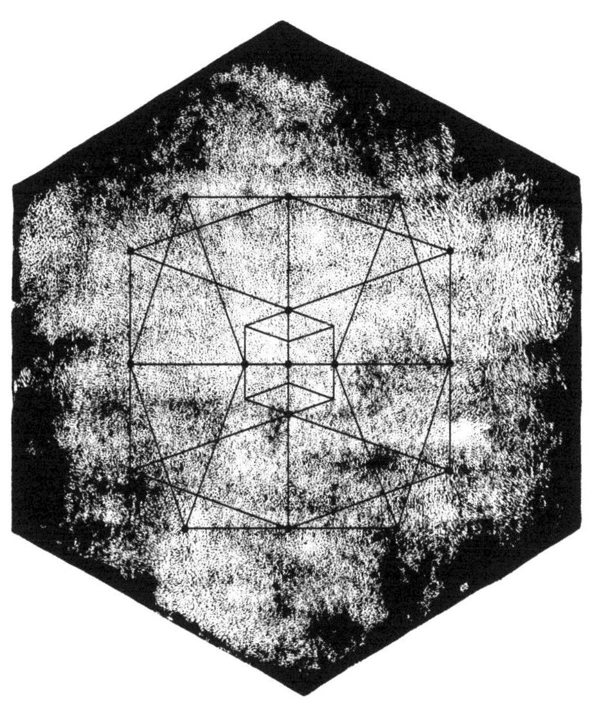

The journey begins with:
"I am alone."
Then it continues with a lovely:
"We are together."
And later, when it clicks, it explodes into
a transcendent sound that travels through all
the levels of existence, a roar that says:
"I AM!"

We are one: Diversity in Unity,
Unity in Diversity.

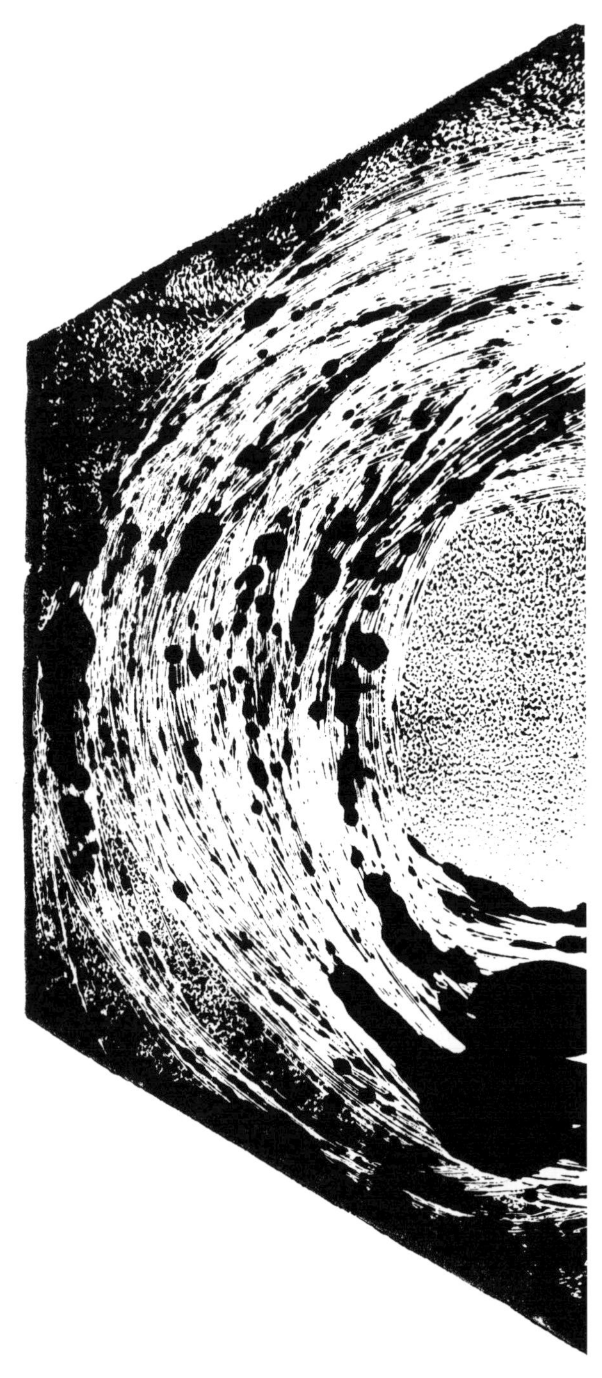

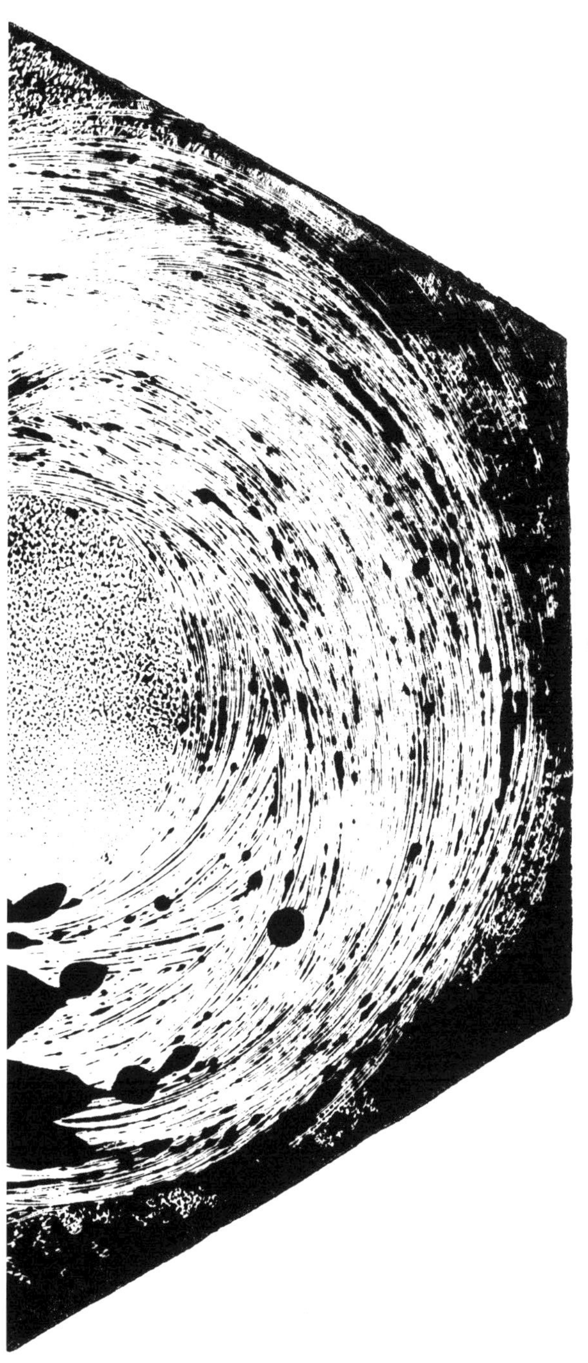

PART 2

REUNION

PATH

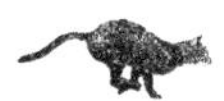

What is Reunion?

In this book, I'm going to share with you a practical approach to spirituality that I call Reunion.

Reunion is a modern practice for spiritual well-being in the modern world. The goal of Reunion, which offers of a set of transformative ideas and practices, is to unfold the reality of the Soul through gnosis (knowledge), the direct experience of the Infinite. Sometimes we call the experience of gnosis "touching the Real," or connecting with ultimate reality.

The title of this book describes what touching the Real feels like, in simple English. When you experience gnosis, you are connecting with the *Super Hyper Vibe!*—a healing, transcendent love energy that allows you to experience every aspect of life on a spiritual level. This means that you are connected with your life, fully present to what is.

Reunion follows the way of knowledge—the path of the initiate, the mystic—which is based on experience. It does this by bringing about the integration of opposites, allowing for a movement from spiritual fragmentation into wholeness.

Because Reunion focuses on the wholeness of human beings in relationship with reality, it combines practices that elevate the Soul (ascending) with active strategies (descending) to create change in the real world. The activation of this dual movement is what makes Reunion unique. (See the workshop in the next chapter.)

In this chapter, I'll share with you some of the Reunion influences, then we'll jump into some key concepts about the nature of reality, the Persona, and the Soul/True Self.

Reunion influences

My creative, seeker friend, as you know, I'm going to insist on keeping Reunion in the "here and the now." In my opinion, it's the only healthy way to talk about spirituality today. But I also feel the need to share with you some of the influences that have helped create and refine Reunion because, although it's new, it is supported and influenced by ancient traditions. Reunion is a contemporary mystical path that follows the insights of initiatory schools such as Western Hermeticism (via ancient Egypt and Greece), Gnosticism, Tantra, and Daoism—to name just a few.

Every religion or philosophy on earth that has a traditional, open path (exoteric) also offers a mystical path (esoteric—hidden). And, historically, it's the mystics, not the clergy, who have discovered the ultimate truth. Mystics find the truth by exploring, not by following the rules/dogmas or by becoming scholars. They do it through direct experience.

Mystics are spiritual rebels. They don't fit in.

When you try to get a sense of their colorful lives, you find

that their insights were so provocative, and so outside the norm, that mystics were more likely to be repressed, excommunicated, or burned at the stake (in Christianity, specifically) than celebrated—even if hundreds of years after their death, they might become canonized (declared saints). Mystics are pushed aside because they are outsiders. That's why you didn't hear about them while growing up. I like to envision mystics as being spiritual artists and visionaries, defiantly dedicating their lives to experiencing spiritual freedom by touching the Real—no matter the personal cost. In an age where lack of commitment is the norm, their dedication is awe-inspiring.

Now, as a spiritual seeker, why did I choose to study multiple mystical paths? Simply because my Soul is curious to explore in order to find the Real. And every religion or philosophical system expresses and points toward the infinite light in a slightly different way. Mystics all talk about the same thing: the universal language of Love.

Another important reason is that, in the past, mystics (to avoid the very real danger of being executed) had the habit of hiding their discoveries through symbols, stories, or even shocking tactics (it was better to look crazy than to face death). And, today, as a student of mysticism, you might reach the limit of one sacred text because it ends abruptly or because a key element has not been included. This is normal—many pearls of knowledge were hidden on purpose. But, interestingly, you might find the missing piece you're looking for in a completely different culture or tradition. When that happens, it's a revelatory moment.

Could creating these types of connections be considered "cultural appropriation"? Maybe. But I don't feel that is the right question. For someone like me, who has lived in three different cultures, has friends all over the world, and has a multicultural family, I can tell you that culture (when it's alive) isn't static at all. On the contrary, it's extremely fluid. It's also interesting to ask whether at any time in human history transformative, life-giving ideas have ever been contained by just one culture. Or do they live beyond it, outside of time and space?

To me, it all comes down to your intent and the discipline of your practice. It's all about your focus on the here and the now, not where you come from.

Here are some questions for you:

Are you just interested? Or are you fully committed?

Are you for real when you're looking for the Real?

Why is the world so messed up?

Okay, so now we're going to jump into our quest for the Real. In our introduction, we've started by looking inward. Together, we saw how the pain in your personal biography could be an entry point into the spiritual journey. Now I'd like you to go outward and look at the world. What do you see? We, the humans: How are we doing on this planet?

When you look at the news, what are your hopes for the future? Are you optimistic or full of fears? Do you find meaning or do you see senselessness? Do you sense spiritual connection or spiritual disarray? Do you see moral strength or moral decrepitude? When you explore social media, do you feel uplifted or drained? Do you think that we're progressing or that we're regressing?

Think about it for a moment, as honestly as you can.

If you really pay attention, you'll find a puzzling, frustrating answer . . .

It's always *both!*

For every horrific event, there is beauty. For every act of hate, there is love. For every lie, there is a truth.

Every extreme finds its opposite.
Every time. Everywhere. *Always.*

Yes, this is frustrating for us human beings, because we are naturally inclined to seek comfort and avoid pain. We all wish life were easier.

But still, why is the world so messed up? If the Creator created this universe, why not create a more balanced environment instead? Why so much friction? Why so much horror and pain?

Unfortunately, these are not the best questions to start understanding the world. Making a fist while screaming at the clouds, "Why, God? Why?" is *not* gonna help.

The first concept here is to accept our limitations (we've talked about this in the introduction). As human beings, we'll never fully understand the whole picture of life, and that's fine. It's good to approach life with humility, knowing that you're dealing with a sacred mystery.

Re-infusing your life with a sense of the sacred is the proper mindset. It might lead you to experience awe, which is an opening for grace. In contrast, the arrogant stance that says,

"I demand all the answers now, or else!" will lead you absolutely nowhere.

Next, it's key to understand that when you're approaching the idea of the Creator, you're dealing with a totality.

The Creator is the ultimate totality. Infinite wholeness.

Because as humans, we are tiny little parts of life (and the Infinite), we can't envision the whole. And we certainly can't comprehend the meaning of the whole (through the mind). However, we can connect with it (through the heart).

Finally, the act of "creating a world" automatically brings polarities/dualities. You can't create one position in space-time without its opposite. If something is small, then something else is big. If something is bright, then something else is dark. If something is blissful, then something else is painful. It never ends. Furthermore, opposites are deeply embedded into one another. If I place an object on a table and light it up with a flashlight, it casts a shadow. The shadow is an automatic by-product of the light. The oneness of light and shadow also helps us see the object better because it is a totality.

So while we'd rather live in an ultra-happy cotton candy universe, that is an impossibility. The material world comes as an integrated duality.

Here, the Daoist Yin-Yang symbol called *Taiji* (太極), showing two opposite forces dynamically joined in a dance, visually represents this totality in motion. Please note the Yin seed inside the Yang, and the Yang seed inside the Yin. *Taiji* is commonly translated as "Supreme Polarity," and the combination of these two words, 太極, can be interpreted as "the source, the beginning of the world."

Modern Taiji "yin-yang symbol"

Based on this insight, you can see that the world might not be so messed up after all. It just *is*. A perfectly balanced totality in motion. What might be messed up, however, is how we interact with it, our stubborn persistence in seeing separation everywhere instead of wholeness.

The human experience of the friction of opposites—no matter how it expresses itself in your life—is exactly where the spiritual initiation can begin. It's a doorway inviting you to discover Infinite Totality and spiritual wholeness.

Plato's cave
[Note: This passage is an extract from my previous book, *You Are a Dream.*]

> In *The Republic*, the Greek philosopher Plato masterfully describes in "The Allegory of the Cave" how we all are prisoners of our own perceptions. In this story, he shows that what we call reality is just a box we live in—a prison we're born into. In this prison/cave, we are looking at a screen, watching a projection of shadows (just like in a movie theater), and we mistakenly believe it's the real thing.
>
> Plato suggests that even if a prisoner were to escape and discover what was really happening outside the prison's walls he would, upon his return, be met with rejection by the remaining prisoners. They would not believe him.
>
> According to Plato, it appears that we love our delusions more than reality.
>
> This idea that the reality we perceive is but a speck of a larger whole is not limited to ancient Greece. It's shared by many cultures and ancient traditions. For example, it's a key concept in Eastern thought, where reality is called *maya*, a Sanskrit word that means "appearance," "illusion," "trick," or "magic." We also find it under a different guise in all shamanic cultures where dreams, or the dream world, coexist side by side and interact with physical reality.
>
> Curiously, men and women of science also recognize

> this idea. David Bohm, one of the most important theoretical physicists and creative minds of the twentieth century, has suggested something similar with his mathematical and physical theory of "implicate" and "explicate" order. And today, many contemporary quantum physicists commonly state that what we call reality (or observer-driven reality) is just one aspect of a much larger, interconnected system/whole.

Okay, let's continue with science a little bit. Reality isn't what we think it is. At the core of the matter, things are not separated as we see them: Everything is one thing. A big soup of energy. This includes our physical bodies, by the way. It so happens that, through our senses, we're converting these signals into a reality where everything is separated. *We* are creating that separation.

Here are some insights from the Australian neurophysiologist Sir John Carew Eccles, who won the Nobel Prize in Medicine for his work on the synapse.

He said, "I want you to know that there are no colors in the real world, there are no fragrances in the real world, that there's no beauty and there's no ugliness. Out there beyond the limits of our perceptual apparatus is the erratically ambiguous and ceaselessly flowing quantum soup.

And we're almost like magicians in that in the very act of perception, we take that quantum soup and we convert it into the experience of material reality in our ordinary everyday waking state of consciousness."

This means that, simply by living, we are automatically translating the experience of life into a subjective thing we call reality.

The word "automatically" is key here. We're doing it without awareness.

Now, a surface understanding of this idea would go like this:

- The world is not what it seems to be.
- My job as a human being is to wake up to the true nature of reality.
- I can meditate a little. See a different perspective.
- Ta-dah! I see we are all interconnected! I've transcended! I can make my own choices! I'm super spiritual! *Namaste!*

Easy!

No.

Here's why.

The four levels of reality

Let's accept the thesis of Plato that we're born into bondage, prisoners inside a cave, watching a big show on a screen called life. Or let's just accept what quantum physicists are telling us: Reality is a big quantum soup of potentialities that we're activating through the act of observation. Now that we know about it, isn't it simple to get out?

Haha! You think?

Not so fast . . .

Plato's cave is the ultimate airtight prison because *WE* are creating it and we are calling this creation "reality." The bondage

is entirely self-created. But it's even deeper than that. Every time we accept this reality at face value, it also creates our sense of self. It goes like this: Your reality creates your sense of self. Your sense of self creates your reality. It's the perfect loop. There's no escape.

Let me give you an example. Let's pretend that you grew up in a very dry, materialistic, unloving environment that sucked the life out of you. At some point in your life, you suddenly say: "That's it!" You completely change your life around new spiritual values. Whereas you used to party hard on a Saturday night, now you're doing meditation retreats. Whereas once you lived in the excess of consumption, now you dress in modest eco-friendly garments. You've made a 180-degree turn.

Or . . .

Did you simply trade one Persona for another without any meaningful transformation?

Ouch!
Again, Plato's cave is no joke.

Let me show you how this works. From our human perspective, this mysterious thing called reality can be split into four levels. Please note: These levels are interconnected, and I'm only splitting them up here for the sake of our conversation.

- Material
- Social
- Psychological
- Archetypal
- Spiritual

The Material level. Everything you can see, smell, touch, and measure. It seems to be very simple and black and white. In Reunion we call it iSTEM: Information, Space, Time, Energy, Matter. Once you start learning about quantum physics (describing the infinitely small), it turns out that the core of the material world is a strange energy soup of potentialities that's influenced by the act of observation. Not so simple after all.

The Social level. As a human being, you are a social animal. Social dynamics rule your life: from the choice of your mate and your interactions with others to your status in the pecking order. You are an interconnected being. You don't exist without others, because they are co-creating you. Your sense of self is not owned just by you, it's collective, because your surroundings always reflect it back to you (social order). The social level is a force that drives constant pressure on the individual to fit within the norm. This pressure leads to the creation of a psychological self, the Persona.

The Psychological level. In this realm things get a little bit more complicated. Feelings, emotions, and interpretations come into play as you translate your material and social reality subjectively. You make judgments about reality by saying: "This is good, and this is bad. She is good, and he is bad." Also, "I am good" or "I am bad." This is the level where you attach characteristics to your sense of self, to define yourself (and the world): "I'm shy." "I'm outgoing." "I'm creative." "I'm scientifically minded." "I'm hurt." "I'm happy." "I love sex." "I hate sex." "I love dancing." "I hate dancing." "I have no power." "I'm powerful." Most of this psychological labeling is based on past experiences. Therefore, your psychological self is entirely past-centric. This is a very big problem because, if you live in the

past (psychologically), you will be entrapped by it. You won't be able to see the possibilities of the present moment.

In our conversation, we call this psychological self the Persona. And while this is the image we identify the most with, the Persona isn't "you" (your Soul/True Self), but a by-product of your experience of life. At the psychological level, the Persona reinforces itself daily by taking fixed positions on anything and everything and cultivating a superb sense of self-righteousness. The Persona automatically creates your identity, your values, your beliefs, your behaviors, and later, your results in life. Therefore, the Persona is the root of all human suffering. But paradoxically, in the spiritual perspective, the Persona is also the key to revealing the Soul.

The Archetypal level. Archetypes are classic characters in stories (orphan, warrior/hero, evil king/queen, wise old man/woman, trickster, etc.) that are universally present in mythology. In the modern era, the psychiatrist Carl Jung uncovered that human life is deeply influenced by these archetypal forces. In Western Esoteric schools, these archetypes are seen as living ideas that are running the show in the background, on automatic.

The Spiritual level. The level of the Soul. You are a Soul having a human experience. Your Soul is not your personality—it is a spark of the divine having a little journey in the here and the now. It is your real "you."

Okay, now that we've explored these four levels of reality, you could say:

"Great, now what?"

Well, let's pause a little bit.

The hardest thing to realize is how automated the entire human experience is. What these four levels suggest is that you are not the free being you think you are; instead, what you "are" is an ongoing process that involves the whole physical world, psychological and archetypal influences, all combined into one neat little Plato's cave package called reality.

All of your problems are not "yours," in that sense. They are happening to this thing you call "you." Which is itself an ongoing process, a by-product of billions upon billions of influences, *not* a fixed thing.

Here, I'm calling this automated self your "Persona." And no matter how cool (or not cool) you think you are, you can't really claim your Persona as being yours, just as a droplet of water in the sky cannot claim to be the whole rainbow. You are, at best, co-participating in a process that's infinitely bigger than you, and this process is creating your Persona. Note: For additional thoughts on the Persona, please read *You Are a Dream.*

This statement is very hard to digest for most people because functionally and culturally we're so used to linking who we are with the Persona.

Early on, I've shared with you how psychological work is important before our journey. Yet the field of psychology is entirely based on the Persona. And its goal is to help make the Persona manageable in the real world. But psychology never questions the reality of the Persona to begin with, to see if—beyond it—there's such a thing as a human Soul/True Self. Why? Because in traditional clinical psychology, there's no

In order to keep you trapped inside Plato's cave, the Persona wants to convince you that your sense of self and reality are completely static. Should you listen to what it says?

human Soul. The Soul and the possible existence of an Infinite Creator are seen as fallacies.

Now, from a mystic's perspective, psychology is a fantastic introductory tool to reveal the games of the Persona; but it is also, interestingly, a field that completely misses the spiritual nature of the human experience. And while therapy can be a first step to awareness, it can become a dead-end long term. Attempting to fix the Persona to make it more integrated might seem to be a great goal, but it's a misguided one. Ultimately, it doesn't work as well as advertised. And when you talk with therapists with decades of clinical work behind them, there is a deep sense of frustration across the board. No real transformation really occurs. Patching up the Persona brings more Persona. This is Plato's cave at its finest.

Based on this perspective, it's not hard to understand why we, the silly humans, are so senseless and, generation after generation, seem to make very little to no progress. When everyone is being run by their Persona, everything is always happening automatically. Even when on the surface positive change seems to occur, as in our previous example in which someone "decides" to move from consumerism to experiencing mindful living, it is still the Persona at play.

There's a great moment in the New Testament where Jesus says, "Father, forgive them, for they do not know what they are doing" (Luke 23:34).

This is very poignant because, in many ways, the story of Jesus is also, symbolically, the story of the shining light of awareness (truth) in friction against the status quo. In a world populated by Personites, truth is dangerous and must be suppressed.

Yet, from the mystic's perspective, humans can't be blamed for their ignorance and must be loved, no matter what. This is a powerful teaching.

You have to learn to accept others completely so you can learn to accept yourself completely as well. Compassion is key. Leaving behind the Persona (which is an illusion to begin with) in order to reveal the reality of the Soul in this human existence is the goal of the spiritual path. It is the only way out of Plato's cave. It is the way of spiritual transformation and freedom.

There's a famous spiritual adage that elegantly expresses this concept:

"We are not human beings having a spiritual experience.
We are spiritual beings having a human experience."

Hard questions

Now let's hit some very hard questions:

As a seeker, can you be bold enough to consider that your seeking might also be part of the shenanigans of Plato's cave? Could your "seeker personality" just be another facet of the Persona? Something that just happened automatically, in reaction to the ongoing narrative of your life?

Now, let's take a deep breath, because here comes the kicker:

"Would you be willing to let go of this "seeker Persona"?

I know I'm asking a lot here, but this is it!

Remember, I've warned you at the beginning of this book. I've

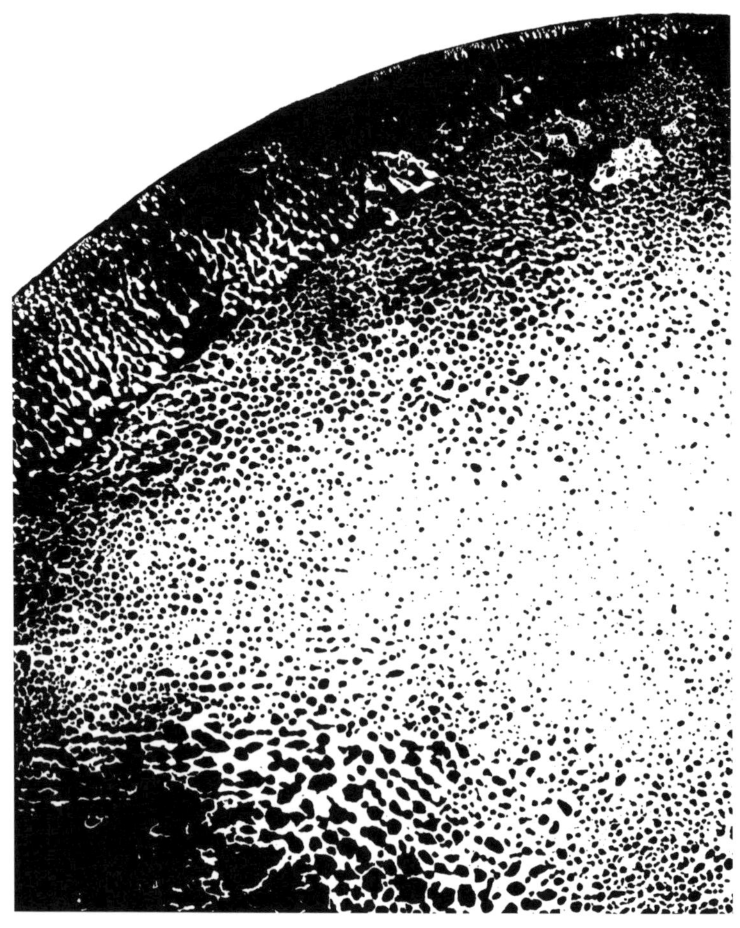

told you that I would challenge you like you've never been challenged before. Well, there you go.

You are a lovely person who has made incredible changes to practice mindful living. I know you have a good heart. You bought this book because you're curious about exploring new ideas. You are a seeker and that's wonderful. And now, I'm asking you: "Can you let go of this seeker Persona?" And here, we're clear that it is implied that this seeker Persona might be complete B.S. (a Boring Subterfuge).

Now you may start boiling and explode: "How rude is that! Are you implying that I am a fake?" (No, I'm not.) "Do you even know all the challenges I went through?" (No, I don't.) "Who the f—k are you, Prof. G?" (I'm no one special.)

Spiritual drama!

Listen, if my directness makes you feel uncomfortable, it means I've got your attention. It also means that we're touching something real together. And now . . . this is the moment we've been waiting for: You're finally ready to close this book and run away!

Or maybe, wait! Just a second . . .

Again,

Would you be willing to let go of this seeker Persona? And if you did, what would suddenly become available for change?

You know the answer.
Everything.

Free will or destiny?

A classic philosophical question is the battle between free will or predestination. As humans, are we free to direct our lives or are we following our destiny?

A few decades ago, as a young twentysomething, I would have been delighted to argue for the side of free will, because I've always used the freedom available in my life to make impactful decisions that led me in new directions. So simple, right?

Now, much older and perhaps a tiny little bit wiser, I know that I actually did not understand the big picture.

In the Arabic world, there's a saying, *maktūb* (مكتوب), which translates as "It is written" and simply means "destiny." Here, the idea is that the Creator/God has already written the script for your life and your goal is to follow this script as well as you can.

Unfortunately, this philosophical position is often misunderstood, and is sometimes used as an excuse to justify apathy and mediocrity. If everything is already written, then why would you even bother trying? That's why in the Western world most people prefer to adopt the "free will" model to conduct their lives.

But . . . is it *that* simple?

The big misunderstanding with predestination is that it's assumed to be one single way—one destiny. But when you're dealing with an Infinite Creator, isn't it safe to assume a destiny containing unlimited possibilities?

I know that this idea is a bit paradoxical, and it should come as no surprise, because, as mentioned before, on the spiritual path of the mystic we're going to see many paradoxes. But—think about it—it's an elegant solution that reconciles the problem of free will versus destiny once and for all.

In Reunion, we're going to look at a destiny with infinite possibilities. This allows for the natural human desire to create, yet it also removes a great weight from your shoulders by also introducing a powerful spiritual practice: surrendering.

Surrendering: a great spiritual secret

To elevate my mood, I love to listen to music. My go-to genres are electronic music, soul, eighties pop, seventies rock, and folk, to name just a few. To me, music is food for the Soul. I feel extremely blessed to live in an era where all the music in the world is available on my phone. This is incredible to me. And I love to explore new musical frontiers I'm unfamiliar with. Recently, I've discovered gospel music, specifically the work of the incredible Andraé Crouch. Part of his body of work is his version of the classic *I Surrender All*, a beautiful song about surrendering.

Surrendering, or letting go, is an extremely important spiritual practice, but perhaps one of the most misunderstood.

In Christianity, surrendering is often described as letting go of your desires and offering your will to God. This allows for an instant lifting of the burden of life while simultaneously putting you where you should be: in the here and the now. That's great.

In Daoism there's the concept of *Wu Wei* (無爲), commonly

described as non-action. In the spiritual state of *Wu Wei*, you completely let go of trying, and instead, practice action-non-action. You're allowing harmony to spontaneously realize itself through you. Again, great.

Whatever your approach to spirituality, the practice of surrendering is amazing.

But, from a mystic's perspective, this is just a first stage, as there is a deeper level to surrendering.

On the path of the mystic, true prayer is gratitude. Gratitude with all your heart for the life you have been given. This is the ultimate form of prayer and should be a daily practice.

Simply say:

> *Dear God/Infinite Creator,*
> *I am deeply grateful to be alive.*
> *I am grateful for life on this earth.*
> *I'm grateful for experiencing it all.*
> *Thank you.*

Please make sure you feel it, as you say these words.

This is just an example—you can use whatever words of your choosing to express this idea of gratitude. But, truly, this is the only prayer you need.

Why?

Because gratitude is an act of love moving outward. It's also an act of remembrance that originates from your core and con-

nects you directly with life and the Infinite. From this perspective, you're not a "beggar" trying to get something out of God (typical Persona B.S.); instead, you are expressing thankfulness for the gift you already have: being a Soul having a human experience. This is key.

In one of my little books of quotes, *You Are a Message*, I wrote:

> Life is waiting for you
> To fall in love with life,
> So life can fall in love with you.

Yes, it's your job to send out indomitable love into your life. That's how you will create this connection with the Creator that will light up your reality with initiatory living. And here's how to do it.

Let's go back to our gospel song, *I Surrender All.* The title of the song reveals an important spiritual secret.

The secret is in this word: "all."

Total surrender.

This means surrendering your life, but more important, it also means surrendering your Persona.

Completely letting go of the socially constructed image of your "self"—this fixed image you attach so much value to—is the great secret. Surrender this Persona and everything that comes with it back to the Creator. This is the scariest thing, but it's the most revolutionary spiritual gesture you can make. It is the path to true freedom.

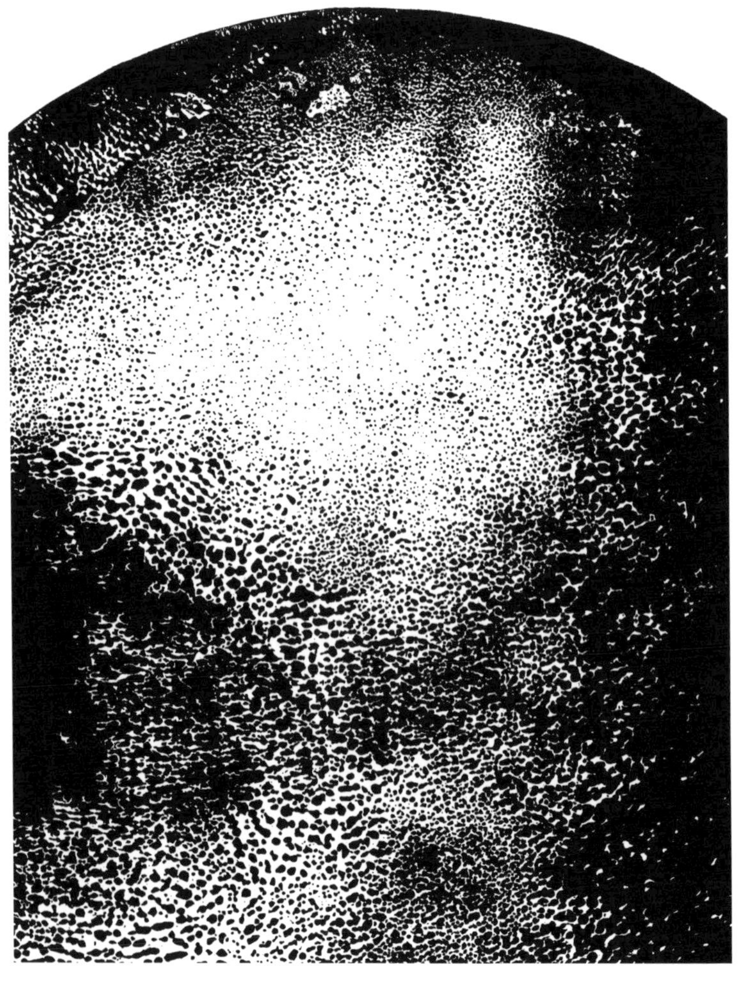

This idea is not new; for example, it's at the root of Zen Buddhism, where the goal of the practitioner is to let go of the "ego self." And the twist here is that this ego self is a complete illusion to begin with. Hence, the keyword here: "remembrance." By letting go of the Persona, you also remember that you are a living Soul traveling through this plane of existence.

And this is why I'm going to repeat myself, one more time, just in case you've missed it. This is for you, my friend:

Would you be willing to let go of this seeker Persona? And if you did, what would suddenly become available for change?

Try it!

Surrender.

All.

Surrendering as initiation

Surrendering (the self, the identity, the history, the pain, the moment) is an experiential spiritual process, not an intellectual one. It can be the most important initiation in your life. By letting go and letting the present be, you can open the spiritual dimension in your life. In an instant.

Here I'd like to share with you how it unfolded during one of the most painful moments of my life.

When my wife and I got pregnant with our first child, we were ecstatic. The pregnancy was a breeze. It was beautiful and exciting to see that our love would soon be expressed into a new human life. *So magical!* And when it was time to go to the hospital for the delivery, we were full of giggles. So happy . . .

But then everything shifted. It happened so fast. The first nurse said: “I can’t find the heartbeat.” Something was wrong. Then, the second nurse: “I don’t hear anything.” And finally, the doctor: “There’s no heartbeat. I’m sorry for your loss.” And that was it.

I can’t even begin to explain the level of hurt of a situation like this. And on that day, I completely lost it. I started ranting at the Creator/God, saying how unjust this moment was. I was angry and devastated.

A nurse, seeing my erratic behavior, popped in and asked my wife if I needed medication to calm me down. And I thought, “Yes! Bring all the pills!” as I would have swallowed an entire bucket of drugs to make the pain go away and fall into deep oblivion. But, out of nowhere, my wife gave me the greatest gift as she replied to the nurse with complete assurance, “No, no pills for him. He’s going to be fine, thank you.”

I was shocked, but this was the push I needed to let go of despair and come back into the present moment. So, with nowhere to hide, we both surrendered to the now—this horrific now. And something happened. Reality shifted.

I wrote about this experience a few weeks later. The following is an extract from a speech I gave for a gathering to thank our friends who supported us during this time:

> As Joanne was going through labor, I looked at her and realized how much I loved her—how beautiful she was. I told her: ‘You’re so beautiful. I love you so much.’ As I held her hand while she gave birth I felt love like I never felt it before. When baby Sophie came—a beautiful, beautiful baby—I was overwhelmed by the pain.

Giving birth to a lifeless baby is the hardest paradox there is. But I stayed present, I stayed present. And something deeper unfolded.

After we were left alone with the baby, something changed in the room. Peace settled in. Then everything started to vibrate . . . and, out of nowhere, a giant wave of Love fell upon us. A Love transcendent, a Love that encompasses everything, a Love that burns, a Love beyond comprehension.

Here we were, alone with our beautiful lifeless baby, surrounded by an incredible energy—a concentrated form of Life.

That day, we were both touched by something bigger than ourselves. We were touched by Love in the most profound sense of the word. And this experience was an initiation into what Life *is*.

And today, I can confess humbly that all my life I've been asking the wrong question:
"What's the meaning of life?" is not the right question.
The right question is "What is Life?"
And this is a hard question because we already know the answer, and we wish it were different.

Life is both:
Life and Death
Joy and Sorrow
Love and Hate
Beauty and Ugliness
Form and Formlessness
Youth and Old Age
Focus and Distraction

Happiness and Sadness
and so on . . .
Life is an ongoing stream of endless opposites we can't seem to reconcile and these are the source of all our sufferings.

But today I can tell you one thing: Yes, Life is *both* the most beautiful thing you can imagine and it can be the most tragic—all at once. But if you stay present—like your life depends on it—in the full awareness of what is, and if you use all you've got to hold these contradictions together and hold them both in full awareness, then you may find that behind this apparent duality there's just one thing: the oneness of Love.

And today, I want to leave you with this idea:

Life (with a big 'L') is
Love (with a big 'L')
Life is Love.
Life is Love.

Now, this moment became a teacher for us during the process of grief. Understanding that the pain we were experiencing was proportionate to the amount of love we were sharing became a life-saver for us. This gave us the strength to stay together, and to find the courage to try again. Which led us, about a year later, to the birth of our daughter, Margaux.

But, there's more . . . Because, unlike in cheesy Hollywood movies with a happy ending, life is a really tough teacher.

Just twelve days after Margaux was born, we noticed she had a

high fever. We immediately took her to the E.R. There, a nurse spotted a tiny zit on her back. Within minutes, this zit doubled in size. Then, tripled. After an hour, it had grown to the size of a backpack. It was horrific. Margaux had caught a staph infection and her vital stats were falling. She was dying.

Now, from the Persona's perspective, you could say: "How unfair is that! How cruel!" But this is not the right response.

And during the three-week battle in the ICU to save our daughter's life, we only talked about love. The gratitude for the love we had at that moment, in the here and the now. We didn't know what the outcome would be but we had complete clarity that this new challenge would never stop us.

Never.

And this time, I did not "lose it," and I did not feel the need for any pills to calm me down. We brought all the love we had in the moment. And we surrendered to it. We accepted that our daughter might not make it. And we loved her for every single second we could spend with her. We brought her as much love as we could, as the doctors pumped her up with the most potent antibiotic cocktail they could find.

And luckily, it worked.

Miraculously, she bounced back into life. And now, eight years later, Margaux is a happy, healthy, and smart little girl with a tiny scar on her back.

Surrendering to what is, while infusing the present moment with your Soul power by bringing unconditional love to any

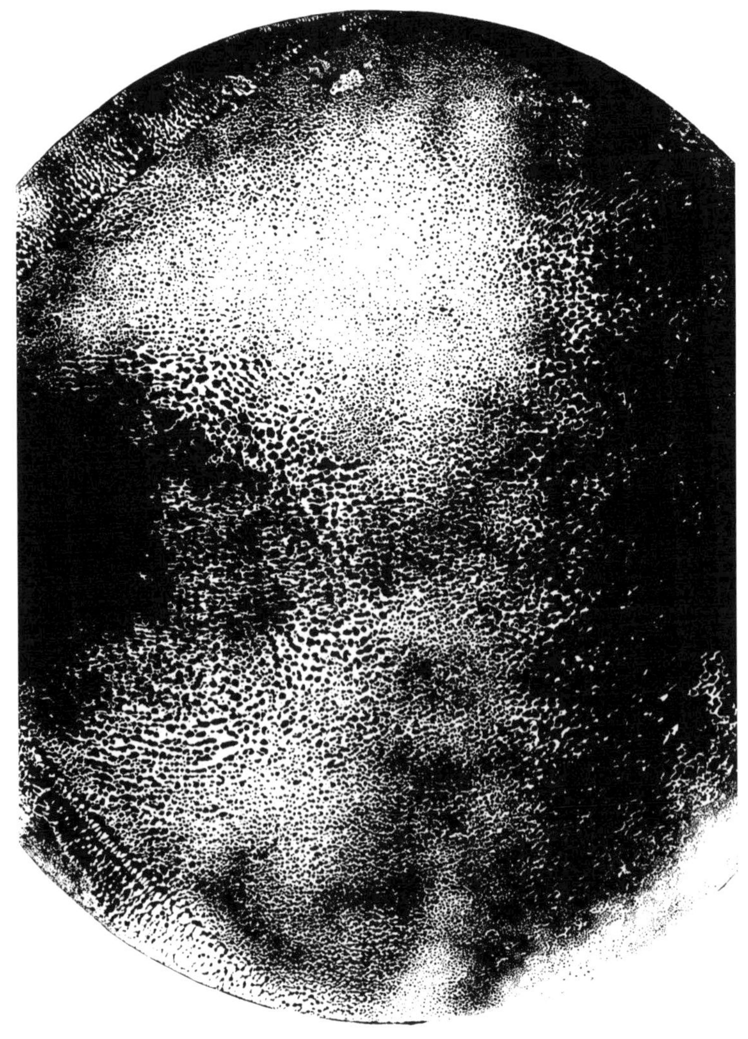

situation, is the warrior stance of the mystic. And it's the only way to live.

Spiritual life isn't about creature comforts; it's about revealing courage and character through Soul power. Touching the Real means getting burned by the fire of living and coming back, whole, through gratitude. Touching the Real also means never taking a simple moment for granted, and instead, infusing your energy in every situation or encounter by being fully present. It means treating every second of living as a gift.

You are here to reveal your Soul by becoming a conqueror of life. A conqueror of the moment. And every single day is an opportunity to do so. This is what spiritual revolutionary living is all about.

The Super Hyper Vibe of the mystic is a state of unity that is experienced with presence through either pain or ecstasy; which are actually different sides of the same coin. Bringing back seemingly complete opposites into the present, then experiencing the friction of these opposites as wholeness: This is how you enter into the Reunion path.

Letting go of all the fears

Once you start surrendering all, including your Persona, and you make that the core of your practice, you automatically put yourself in direct conflict with your fears. Because now, from the Persona's perspective, the game is on.

You see, the Persona isn't going to disappear without a good fight. And the more you bring intensity to your practice, the more the Persona is going to attempt to send you back into Plato's cave. This is done through fear.

Sometimes I like to compare the Persona to a computer virus. A hidden code that runs a program without the user's awareness. A ruthless little program that doesn't want to go away. Here I'm going to tell you a real-life story to illustrate how ruthless the Persona can be, but I'm going to change some details to protect the person's privacy.

A long, long time ago, I was working on a social change project, part of a class I was teaching. We were helping a nonprofit whose goal was to serve an underprivileged community known for its gang activity. In my class, I had a student we're going to call James, who immediately struck me as having a Persona conflict. Here we were, working on this project, and instinctively, I could feel something was a bit off with him. Everything he said, his work, and general attitude was very positive, but I sensed it might just be a front.

Yet I decided to cast away my doubts; after all, I'm not a mind reader, and as a teacher it's an absolute must for me to never judge a student.

A few weeks into the class, the time came to go on a field trip to the city. The trip was organized and guided by local stakeholders in the project, so even though the city was notorious for its crime rate, there was no real danger involved. Yet, as we came closer to the date, James became more and more agitated. He started questioning the safety of the trip. Then, he burst out that he knew that he was being irrational. I could see he was battling with a silent, inner struggle.

One day, he suddenly confessed that he was terrified of the trip. He told us that he had been raised in a racist family environment where he had been told since childhood that people of color were out there to get him. It was a painful, sad moment as he broke out in tears, sharing this to his friend in the class, who happened to be a young black man.

Unfortunately, on the day of the trip, James did not show up. His Persona, simply by using fear, won. To this day, I feel this was a missed opportunity for him to grow spiritually, because I know very well that at the core of his Soul he was full of love. Not hatred or fear. But I also understand how, in this instance, his Persona was able to control his emotions, thoughts, and actions.

You see, the work we're talking about here is hard. Letting go of your Persona is easier said than done. But the price for not doing the work is living your life as a prisoner of your own fears. Fear is what's keeping Plato's cave up and running. Do you want that? Of course not! Walking the spiritual path demands that you confront your fears, because that's how you can truly let the Persona go.

And this is why, in Reunion, we're going into the world to allow for the friction of reality to occur. Touching the Real means stepping outside of your comfort zone through action.

The Persona's game

If the goal is to get rid of the Persona in order to let your Soul/True Self shine, how do you do it?

The Persona uses mimicry and is an expert at impersonating you, saying things like "I can't ever be happy! I don't deserve good things!" At first, it's not really easy to uncover the Persona because it uses this "little voice" in your head that you're so used to and that you trust to be you.

Yet there are two things that are unique about the Persona's expression that reveal the con. Spotting them is how you uncover the Persona's game:

1 • The Persona always speaks in absolutes, as in the previous example: “I can’t ever be happy! I don’t deserve good things!” Observe these statements. They do not allow for anything but extremes. If you spot these absolutes, you need to probe:

- According to whom?
- What would happen if you did?
(A: You would change! See below.)
- How do you know you can’t?
- How do you know it’s forever?

Question these absolute thoughts coming from the Persona, and be ruthless with their ridiculousness! Push as hard as you can! *Mock them!*

2• The Persona always wants to keep things (and yourself) the same, at all cost.

Remember, the Persona is based on the past and doesn’t want you (or your life) to evolve and grow. Why? Because the more you grow into the reality of your Soul/True Self, the more the Persona disappears. Obviously, the Persona is against it! Simple. You can spot a Persona’s statement because it will always imply the impossibility of change. Look at our examples “I can’t ever be happy! I don’t deserve good things!” and you’ll see that both imply that change is impossible. But, as we already know, life *is* change. You can’t experience life fully without inviting change into your life.
You should train yourself to spot the Persona. When negative ideas pop in your mind, ask yourself:

- Is this an absolute?
- Is this preventing change and growth?

And if the answer is yes, on both counts, then you've got a Persona statement. Here I'm going to give you an example. A few years ago I met a talented artisan and I was exchanging ideas on how he could grow his business. Very quickly, I sensed that he was a bit uncomfortable with our conversation. I probed a little and he told me:

"You know, I don't like money. It always brings out the worst in people."

How about that for a nice Persona statement!

So here, you could use these questions:

- According to whom?
(A: past voices, parents, or teachers.)
- How do you know it's "always" the case?
(A: You don't.)
- What would happen instead if money could bring out the best in you?
(A: You would be forced to grow.)

But here I asked him a very provocative question instead:

"Oh, yeah? I can see that, with bank robbers and so on . . . But how about love, then? Are you against love as well? Because when you look at crimes, a lot of stories are crimes of passion. Do you think love really brings out the worst in people as well?"

You see, that's how you push the Persona into a little corner. Life isn't about absolutes. You can't really say that love or money is absolutely bad. You can't really say they are abso-

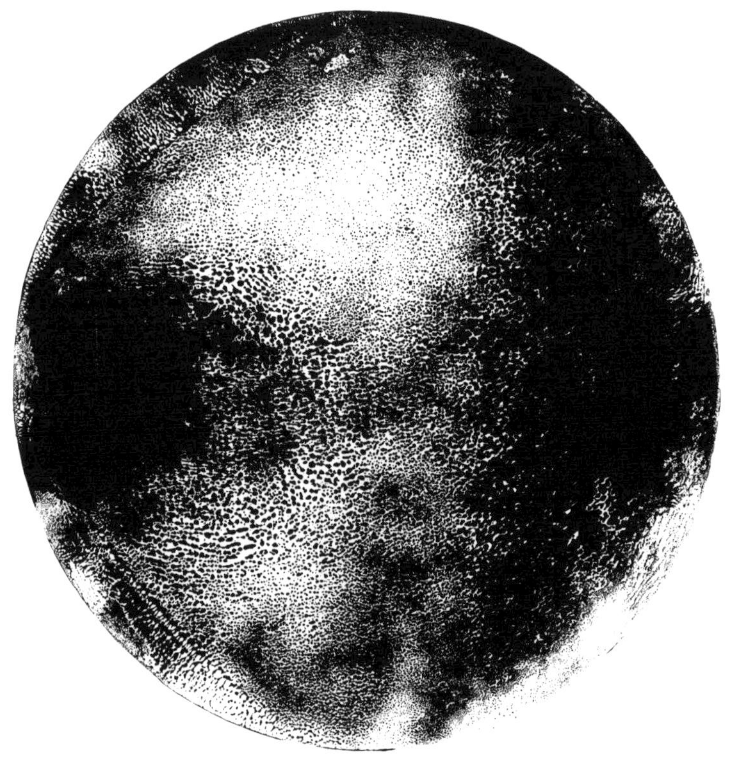

lutely good either. They are completely neutral. But when you take a rigid stance by associating something with an absolute, you freeze yourself into a position where you will not be able to grow anymore. And that's exactly what your Persona wants: to keep you in your comfort zone.

Frozen. *Always*.

Now let's play a game to see what your Persona is all about. Answer as honestly as you can to the following questions. Don't overthink it—go with your gut reaction. Ready? *Go!*

Money: Good or bad?
Love: Good or bad?
Friendships: Good or bad?
Work: Good or bad?
Sex: Good or bad?
You: Good or bad?
People: Good or bad?
Your city: Good or bad?
Your country: Good or bad?
Life: Good or bad?
Food: Good or bad?
Knives: Good or bad?
Guns: Good or bad?
Spoons: Good or bad?
Cars: Good or bad?
Public transportation: Good or bad?

Did you find any absolutes in your answers? I purposefully chose a few good ones that should get your Persona agitated! However, from a mystic's perspective, the answers to these questions are always: *Neither*.

Money is neither good nor bad; it can be used for both. The same with the rest of the list.

Why did I add spoons to the list? Am I being ridiculous? Not at all. We all use spoons for eating, and that's obviously good. But unfortunately, for a drug addict who's a heroin user, the spoon is an instrument that's used daily to destroy the addict's life. So now, is a spoon an instrument of death or sustenance? Neither, of course—the spoon is neutral.

The secret here is to discover unity by bringing opposites together. This is extremely hard to do when it comes to the big ones: crime, violence, disease, and death. And this is why I've shared with you my experience of losing a child. Life can be brutal. I know it.

Reuniting opposites isn't a mental trick; it's a way of being in the world that demands Soul power. You must completely surrender to the All that's manifested in the present moment, while simultaneously acting in your life with growth-driven purpose. In Reunion, this dual movement is called ascending/descending.

Reunion is ascending/descending

Do you know the story of Jacob's Ladder? No? Well, here it is:

> Jacob left Beersheba and set out for Harran. When he reached a certain place, he stopped for the night because the sun had set. Taking one of the stones there, he put it under his head and lay down to sleep. He had a dream in which he saw a stairway resting on the earth, with its top reaching to heaven, and the angels of God were ascending and descending on it.

Then, Jacob has a conversation with God. And later:

> When Jacob awoke from his sleep, he thought, "Surely the Lord is in this place, and I was not aware of it." He was afraid and said, "How awesome is this place! This is none other than the house of God; this is the gate of heaven." (Genesis 28:10–17)

From a mystic's perspective, this story is packed with esoteric (hidden) knowledge. This is the story of a Soul's initiation. First, Jacob finds an entrance into Infinity. In his vision, he is connected with the ultimate reality, the gate of heaven. But in order to reach this ultimate reality he sees that the angels are using the ladder in a dual movement: both ascending and descending on it.

This upward/downward direction is the first secret teaching in this story, the "how-to" into Infinity, so to speak. It's also a core principle of the Reunion path.

In spirituality, there are many practices that only have an ascending nature: prayer, meditation, mantra chanting, fasting, etc. In these practices, the goal is to quiet the mind and elevate the Soul through detachment from thoughts and the concerns of the material world. Unfortunately, in itself, this could lead to creating a new "I'm very spiritual" Persona. Most spiritual practices fall into this trap by inciting their practitioners to ascend, ascend, ascend! The more detached, they say, the more spiritual you are. Is this really true? *Maybe*.

But if you ascend too high, you might lose your capacity to be connected with the world. If you can achieve happiness only while meditating, which is about one percent of your time, does it mean that the remaining ninety-nine percent of your day you're just experiencing constant frustration because the world brings you back down?

On the other hand, it's mostly in the world of self-development that you see descending practices: Get your life together! Learn to be more social by going out! Exercise and eat good food! Get your accounting and finances together! Start your own business! Here, the idea is that, in order to win the game of life, you are going to descend into the material world to create change through willpower and hard work. Does it work? Yes, of course. But the danger is completely losing your Soul connection in the search for material success by becoming a slave to duality. In everyday language this is called "getting caught up in the rat race" or falling for the "hustle culture."

The secret is to bring about the reunion of both currents: To reveal the Infinite in your life, you need to simultaneously ascend *and* descend.

The second insight from Jacob's story is revealed when he says: "Surely the Lord is in this place, and I was not aware of it." This is a call to practice awareness. If you're asleep to the reality of the Soul, you will miss it. Conversely, if you bring your whole attention to the present moment, the higher dimension of your life will be presented to you. Right here, right now.

This idea, where the mystic has to ascend and descend simultaneously, is not unique to the story of Jacob's Ladder and Judeo-Christianity. We also find it under different guises, in the tradition of Kashmir Shaivism. In *The Aphorisms of Śiva*, translated by Mark S. G. Dyczkowski (1992, SUNY Press), we discover that it is:

> "The absolute which pours out of itself as the supreme power of consciousness. Its throb is the pulsing union of Śiva and Śakti through which the universe is eternally emitted and reabsorbed as it expands and contracts." And later we learn that for the yogi, "the Heart, in this context, is understood to be the point of contact between ascending and descending currents of the breath, that in the contemplative absorption which results when the activity of the mind is suspended, are withdrawn into it."

Now let's move to another tradition. In Hermeticism, there's a classic text called *The Emerald Tablet*, also known as the *Tabula Smaragdina*. This enigmatic work was foundational for European alchemists of the Renaissance, as it describes the secret of the great work (*magnum opus*).

Here are the opening lines:

> "This is true without lying, certain and most true.
> That which is below is like that which is above
> and that which is above is like that which is below
> to do the miracles of one only thing."

This echoes, verbatim, an early Gnostic text, the Gospel of Thomas from the *Nag Hammadi Scriptures* (60 A.D.).

> Jesus said to them, "When you make the two into one, and when you make the inner like the outer and the outer like the inner, and the upper like the lower, . . . then you will enter the kingdom."

In the Gospel of Thomas, we also read,

"The kingdom is inside of you, and outside of you."

To the initiate, the message is clear: "As above, so below"—everything is interconnected in oneness. The way to reveal it is through the dual current of ascending/descending.

But there's more . . .

Exploring this dual current is also an opportunity to discover your true nature. As a human being, *you* are the living fusion between heaven and earth, being expressed through your awakened Soul consciousness.

Meister Eckhart, the celebrated fourteenth-century theologian, philosopher, and mystic, describes this experience when he writes: "The eye through which I see God is the same eye through which God sees me."

The practice of ascending/descending is the entry point into Reunion. It reveals wholeness in life through nonduality. It is the way to unity in diversity, and diversity in unity. It is the key to finding freedom by revealing your Soul Power. But watch out—this practice is not for everyone, as it is set up to challenge the status quo of the Persona. It demands courage, persistence, and hard work.

The adventure begins now!
Now I'd like to invite you to stop reading for a moment. Take a minute to look around you, right now. What do you see?

Are you surrounded by beauty?
Are you living in a house that you truly love?
Or did life nudge you randomly into this place?

Now let's look inside.

- How are you experiencing your life today?
- How's your Persona treating you?
- Are you full of positive creative energy?
- Is your life meaningful?
- Are you inspired and enthusiastic?
- Do you have a higher purpose?
- Or are you dealing with blocks and fears that keep dragging you down, no matter how hard you try?

Now let's look at your social self.

- Do you feel connected with others?
- Do you have love in your life?
- Does your work allow you to grow and evolve?
- Or do you feel you could be, do, and have much, much more?

First, no matter where you are today, please DO NOT JUDGE YOURSELF!

(I'm writing all caps so you know I'm being serious here.)

I'm going to ask you to bring maximum compassion into your life, just the way it is now. Your Persona operates in an ongoing process in which you have very little say. It's like a season. It so happens to happen the way it happens.

Your life *is* a journey and you are here to grow and evolve. And that's how it works for you and everyone else on this planet.

So, *yes*, please bring maximum compassion for yourself and for the rest of humanity.

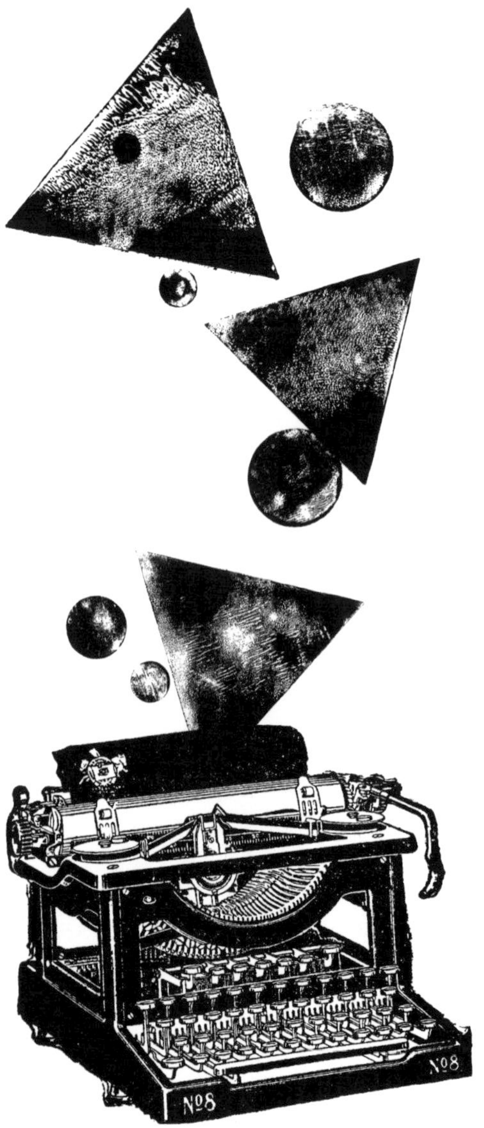

Once you realize that your life is the playground for your Soul, you can start writing a new story that will support freedom, creativity, and love.

Got it? Good.

Be gentle with yourself.

After all, we're clear that this Persona and Plato's cave business is hard. Yes, you may have made millions of mistakes in your life. Yes, there's a side of you that might even be completely self-absorbed, petty, and mean. Ultimately, it doesn't matter—it's just Persona stuff. And you are not alone. Know that everyone else on this beautiful little planet is carrying the same burden.

Yet there's good news because, simultaneously, something very important is also happening:

Your life, as it is now, is also the playground for your Soul.

You are a Soul Being having a human experience.

You really need to hear this message and internalize it.
And so, again:

You are a Soul Being having a human experience.

And, no matter how hard you think it's going to be, you need to realize that the authentic transformation from Persona-based to Soul-based can be experienced in your own life, starting from where you are today.

The moment of transformation itself is instantaneous. And this moment is available to you if you invite it into your life.

It's like turning on a switch. And when it happens, it is the greatest gift you can get: Unconditional spiritual freedom. Complete connection with your life and the lives of others. A deep sense of infinite possibilities to create and experience. Gratitude and love. Feeling whole in a whole world.

And before we move to the workshop part of this book, please know this:

Your life, as it is today, is your great adventure. It might not feel that way to you now, but it is. Whatever frustration, pain, fear, or boredom you might be experiencing at this very moment, this is an opportunity to remember that you are a Soul on a short journey on planet Earth.

You are here on a mission.

This is it!

Listen. This great adventure is not something that will happen tomorrow: It's happening now.

Yes, right now, as you're reading these lines!

Are you ready to connect with the ultimate Super Hyper Vibe that your Soul is craving?

Yes?

Let's do it.

For every horrific event, there is beauty.
For every act of hate, there is love.
For every lie, there is a truth.

Every extreme finds its opposite.
Every time. Everywhere. *Always.*

The human experience of the friction of opposites —no matter how it expresses itself in your life— is exactly where the spiritual initiation can begin.

It's a doorway inviting you to discover Infinite Totality and spiritual wholeness.

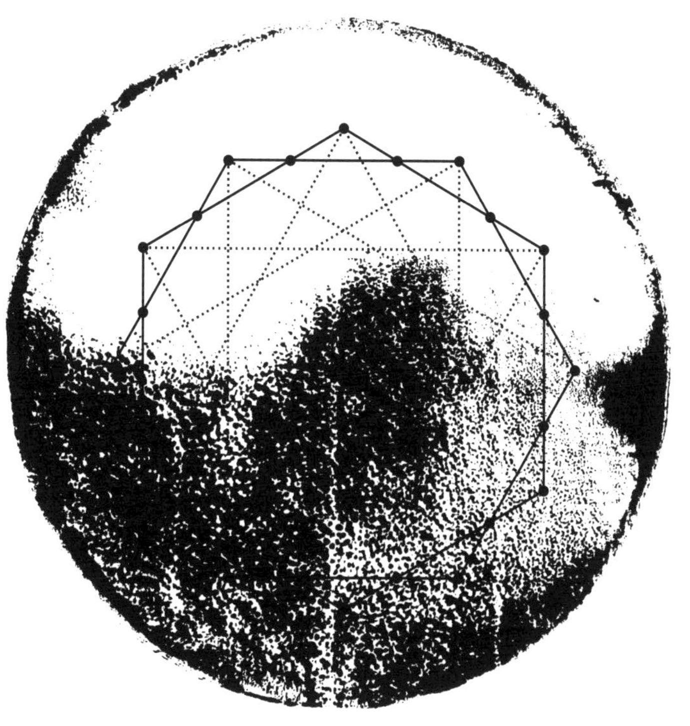

Leaving behind the Persona in order to reveal the reality of the Soul in this human existence is the goal of the spiritual path.

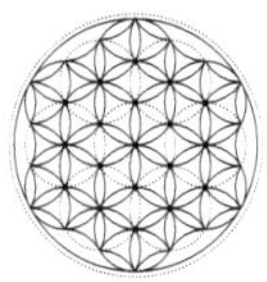

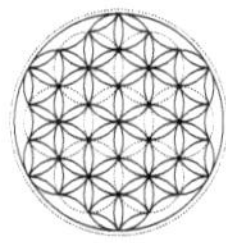

True prayer is gratitude. Simply say:

Dear God/Infinite Creator,
I am deeply grateful to be alive.
I am grateful for life on this earth.
I'm grateful for experiencing it all.
Thank you.

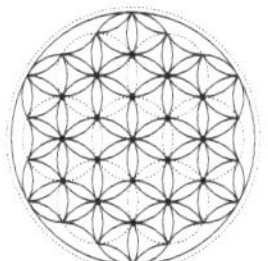

You are here to reveal your Soul by becoming
a conqueror of life. A conqueror of the moment.
And every single day is an opportunity to do so.
This is what spiritual revolutionary living is all about.

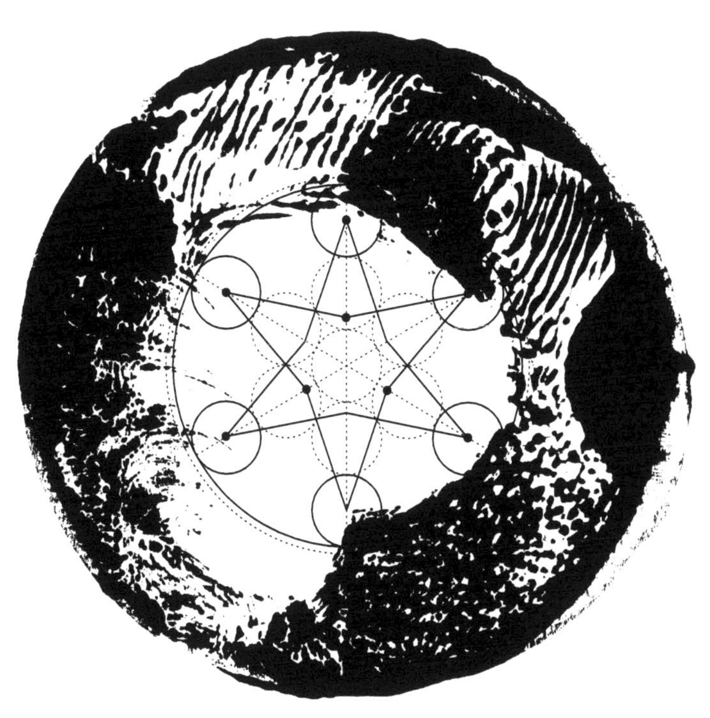

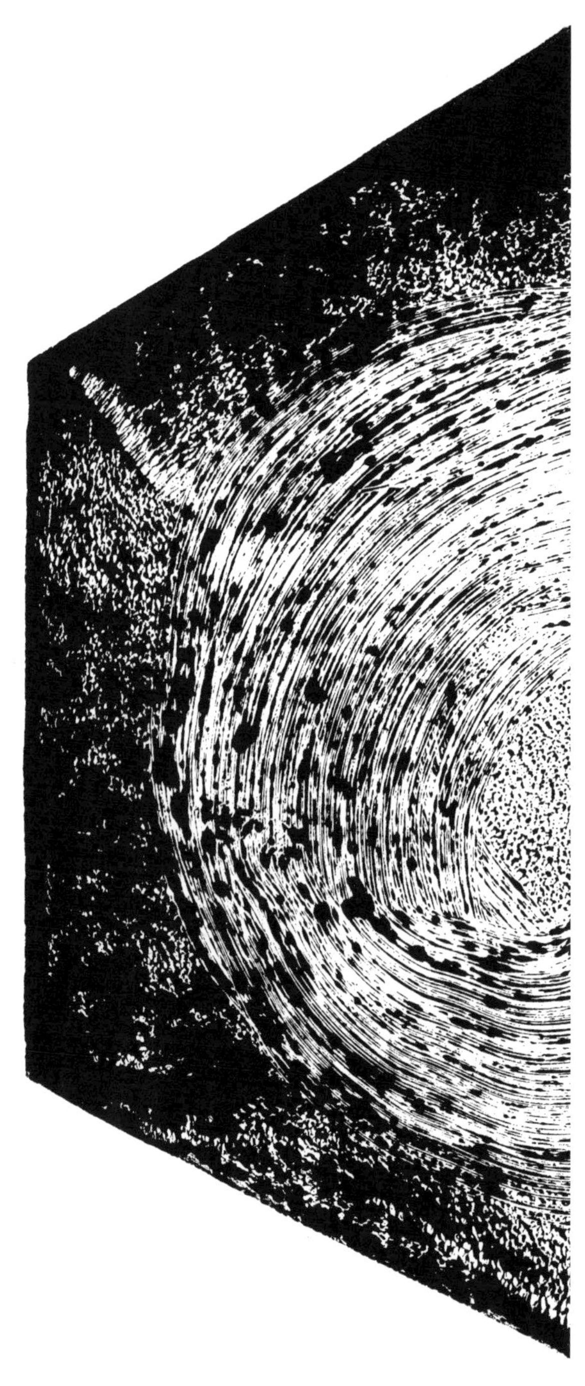

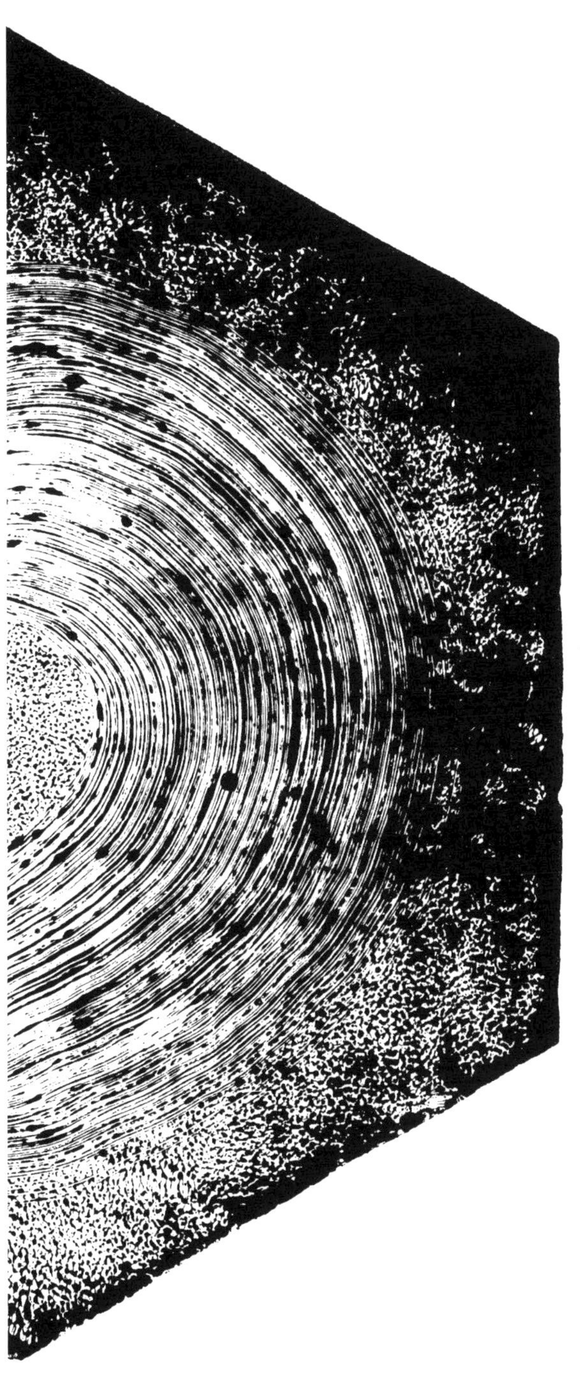

PART 3

WORKSHOP

Welcome to the seven-day Reunion workshop to awaken your Soul.

Now I'd like to invite you to consider this workshop as an experience. This experience will be completely unique for you, but there's a catch: You need to be honest with yourself and willing to go outside of your comfort zone to get the best results.

Do you have to be perfect?

Absolutely not!

Just be you.

In this section, I'm leaving plenty of blank space so you can write down your notes and impressions at the end of each day. Take your time to write these down. This is not something that's meant to be shared, so you can treat it like a personal journal.

What do you need for the seven days?

Because we're going to create some time and space for you, insights and new ideas are going to come up automatically. So I recommend that you also keep a notebook and a pen on you at all times in addition to your phone.

Next, because you're holding a book, which is a little bit of a one-dimensional format, I thought it could be interesting for us to add some video into the mix so we can have a more direct experience.

How does it work? Simple!

•1 Go to this address:

www.profg.co/shv

Or scan this QR code,
using the camera on your phone:

•2 Enter your e-mail address, and start watching!

Hey, do you want to try it now?
Okay, go for it, and check out the introduction:

WATCH VIDEO INTRODUCTION

Great, it's working!

For the next seven days, our goal together is to have you experience:

Day 1: Awareness (focus/no distractions)
Day 2: Energy (connection)
Day 3: Reunion (ascend/descend)
Day 4: Possibilities (creative dreaming)
Day 5: Action (creative gesture)
Day 6: Surrender (gratitude)
Day 7: Meaning (Super Hyper Vibe)

At the end of the workshop, you'll be left with a feeling of openness and possibility. You'll have a new sense of living your life from your Soul/True Self perspective, free of the constraints of Plato's cave and the Persona. A little taste of immanence and transcendence in the everyday! Sound good?

How are we going to make this happen?

Well, first, I'm going to challenge your Persona, of course!

So, here, please understand that in order for you to notice the Persona as being this driving force that controls every aspect of your life, we first need to make you notice that it's there to begin with.

How?

Easy: It's done by creating situations that will force the Persona to react. And nothing makes the Persona react as much as getting yourself outside of your comfort zone, trying new things, questioning the status quo (the willingness to keep things the same), and intentionally creating change.

So together, during these seven days, we're going to tease your Persona, tickle it, and corner it into a place where it can no longer hide.

And here, this is very important: In order for you to succeed, I'm going to ask you to take your Persona with a grain of salt. Humor is key.

In this workshop I'm going to ask you to try certain things and—you'll see—your Persona is going to react, big time: "This is impossible! This is a waste of my time! There's no way I'm doing this!" And so on . . .

This reaction is exactly what we want, because it will help you become the observer of the Persona. And instead of judging it or fighting it, simply look at it with compassion and humor, just as you would if you were to look at a dog chasing his own tail.

Another very important point: There are certain aspects of the workshop that you won't be able to complete on the first try. You shouldn't worry about it, because this is done on purpose.

If you uncover a task you cannot do, please make sure that you listen to your Persona explaining why it's impossible to achieve. Write it down. And then question this statement by asking: "Why not?"

Our goal together is to start a dialogue between your Persona—the conditioned self, which expresses itself through a limiting, past-centric, nagging little voice—and your Soul/True Self, which is unlimited in nature and focused on the present moment.

Ready?

DAY 1 - AWARENESS

As a normal human being living in the modern world—also known as consumer society—every single day you are fighting an invisible battle without knowing it: It's the battle for your attention.

You see, we live in an age called the attention economy, which means that your attention is a commodity that everyone is fighting for. Yesterday, it was done through TV and radio. Today, it's done through your phone, e-mail, and social media. Tomorrow? It might be done through some AR glasses or contact lenses. The day after tomorrow? Maybe brain implants . . .

Yikes!

On a large scale, society operates by influencing you toward following certain directions. Many of these "currents of influence" do not have your best interest at heart. For example, if your banker calls you tomorrow to offer you a personal loan, is this a blessing, or could it be a potential problem? Next, look at your inbox: There's an online sale! For a limited time only you can buy this thing for 50 percent off . . . *Hurry!* Should you press the "buy now" button?

These are very good questions, *right?*

You see, there's a deep connection between the Persona, attention, and consumer society. In a sense, you could say that consumer society always targets the Persona with the promise of instant gratification, love, self-respect, and status.

But because this is done through material acquisitions—things that are outside of yourself—you end up being stuck forever in a hamster wheel. The satisfaction is short-lived; the chase for the fix never stops.

This is the perfect definition of addiction through distraction. The less centered you are, the easier it is to influence you.

And there's more. This ongoing cultural training toward distraction keeps you deep inside Plato's cave, because the more distracted you are, the less introspective you will be.

There's no way you'll get meaningful insights about life or your Soul/True Self if you're in a constant state of distraction.

This negative influence isn't just on the exterior, by the way. It also operates on the inside. Because the Persona has one goal, which is to sustain itself at all costs, it will do whatever it can to keep you unconscious in your daily activities. Through distractions, it will encourage you to fall for all kinds of destructive behaviors, addictions, and bad habits (spiritual, psychological, and biological) that will dampen your capacity to experience your Soul/True Self (awareness). In other words, the Persona is a bit like a stage hypnotist telling you to "stay asleep!" so it can proceed with running your life on automatic.

How to spot the Persona

In *You Are a Dream*, I describe how the Persona operates internally through people, and it's clear that these behaviors have in common a complete lack of awareness.

Unfortunately, the Persona manifests itself in the darkest, ugliest, and saddest human behaviors:

- The husband who physically abuses his wife because he's "right."
- The alcoholic who drinks himself to death because he's "not corrupted, like everyone else."
- The religious fanatic who kills another man—and himself—because he's "on a mission for God."
- The businessman who sells a product that actually destroys the physical health of his customers (or nature), and reassures himself by saying he has "bills to pay and a family to take care of."
- The tourist who drops trash wherever he/she goes because "someone else will pick it up."
- The parent who "beats some sense" into his/her child because he/she "was raised this way."
- The creative who gives up on her art because she's "not good enough, and it's too risky."
- The intelligent soul who never dares to speak up because "speaking up gets you in trouble."
- The workaholic who neglects his family because "this is the price of success."

Today, I could also add to the list:

- The adult-baby pothead, who's stuck playing videogames all day long and spends thousands of dollars on virtual items to get a sense of significance. (Did you know that trading virtual items in videogames is a full-blown, expanding industry?)

- The car fanatic who gets in debt for $250,000 to purchase an exotic car in hopes of—one day–becoming popular on YouTube.

- The mall rat who spends all her money shopping for products she doesn't need to try to impress people she doesn't care about.

- The crazy mom/dad who, during a pandemic, goes into full-blown "locust mode" and empties the shelves of the local supermarket to hoard paper towels and toilet paper. Note: At the time of this writing, the coronavirus crisis has shown us in the most surprising ways how fast the Persona takes over (through fear) and makes people indulge in crazy antics.

The list is infinite. You and I have seen the Persona before, unfortunately, way too many times.

And there's a dire consequence: If, all your life, you stay asleep, only listening to the Persona, you will end up stuck in a space disconnected from life itself—caring only for this illusory image. This image is shallow, divisive, calculating, manipulative, anxious, never satisfied, and prone to temper tantrums if it doesn't get what it wants. It is isolated and lives a meaningless life. You see, the Persona puts you in a game that cannot be won, because this game is being played outside of yourself. The way out is to bring back together the temporal and the eternal by connecting with your inner, spiritual dimension that's infused with meaning.

How?

Realize that beyond your Persona, you are a Soul Being connected with life and the Creator. Live your life from this perspective. This is where total spiritual freedom lives.

Here, of course, one of the greatest tricks of the Persona is to make you believe that this automatically generated image is actually who you are.

For example, let's say that as you follow the Persona's influence, you behave in a way that's either domineering or subservient. Now, if you start saying to yourself, "I'm a winner" or "I'm a loser," you're now attaching a permanent identity to a behavior.

This identity labeling also works when you try to escape from it. As I've mentioned before, if you make some life changes and start calling yourself "a very spiritual person," this new label has the Persona written all over it.

Watch out for this identity B.S.!

The Persona loves to do this because it keeps you stuck. Once the label is attached as an identity, it's game over, because you are crystallizing yourself into a rigid position in space-time.

As someone who works with people, I hear things like this all the time:

"How can I possibly change? After all, this is who I am."

The Persona favors rigidity in identity, not fluidity.

Once this identity is established as a "truth," it's going to be very difficult to change your behavior, because you will act according to your sense of identity.

Here, a brilliant quote from Søren Kierkegaard comes to mind:

"Once you label me, you negate me."

So please, know that it's not what you do—or the situation you're in—that defines who you are. The more unaware and distracted you are in your life, the more likely you are to behave in reaction to your environment. This is simply a temporary, automatic response that isn't a permanent characteristic. Understanding this is key, because this realization opens the door to the possibility for deep transformation.

The greatest philosophical injunction of all time, coming to us from ancient Greece, is still extremely relevant today:

"Know thyself!"

And therefore . . . It's time to wake up!

Okay . . . Your first goal, on day one, is to reclaim your sovereignty by doing a distraction detox.

Why?

Because your capacity to be present for what is without constant distractions is the most direct way to reconnect with your Soul/True Self. Right now, you are being pulled out of your center, daily, and you need to find your core again to return to the here and the now. Distractions are pulling you away from your Soul/True Self—and this is a major problem because:

The present is immanence, and immanence is the gateway into Infinity. That's why being in the awareness of the Now is the most important skill you can cultivate.

So here's what we're going to do for one week: We're going to remove all the distractions your Persona has been using against you in order to keep you deep inside Plato's cave.

And guess what? Removing these distractions is going to make the Persona get mad! And this is exactly what we want.

Distraction detox challenge (for seven days):

> No drugs or alcohol
> No social media
> No videogames
> No news
> No sex (with a partner or solo)
> No added sugar (except for sugar in fruits)

As you read this first assignment, your Persona might jump in and say:

"I can't do this! This is too much! I need my glass of wine at the end of the day!" Or "There's no way I can stop social media because that's how I stay connected with my friends!" Or "There's nothing wrong with sex! My body needs it!"

To which you're going to answer:

"Yes, yes, and yes! Yes, Persona, I get it. You always have great explanations and excuses for everything when it comes to putting me to sleep. That's what you do, *right?*"

You see? Push the Persona back against the wall. Because from your True Self/Soul perspective, you know that you can figure it out and remove these distractions for a week, then succeed with this assignment. It's really not a big deal. If you want to, you can make it work, right? I know you can do it; and you know it, too.

Is it going to be easy, though?

Nope!

Just like waking up from a very long sleep (think Snow White level), it's going to be hard.

Fear not, my friend. Here's a little help:

 **WATCH VIDEO 1 UNAWARENESS DETOX**

END OF DAY 1 - WRITE DOWN YOUR NOTES
(Complete before going to bed):

Please check the boxes next to the distractions you've been able to cancel. But more important, circle the ones that you were not able to get rid of and write down your Persona's explanations/rationalizations:

No drugs or alcohol [YES/NO]
No social media [YES/NO]
No videogames [YES/NO]
No news [YES/NO]
No sex (with a partner or solo) [YES/NO]
No added sugar [YES/NO]

Today, I'm successfully taking a seven-day break from:

And I can do it because:

However, I can't let go of:

And my Persona suggests it's impossible to get rid of these, because it says:

In reality, from my Soul/True Self perspective—if my life depended on it—I could totally succeed if I really wanted to, and I even know how I would do it. I would do it like this:

Now that I know which distraction(s) I apparently can't get rid of (for now), what's the payoff for keeping these active?

Tip: The Persona's payoff always seems caring, as in "You will not be disappointed again. It will protect you from getting hurt. Life is more fun this way!" and so on. But there's a catch: In exchange, you'll get stuck in a frozen stage where you won't be able to grow and evolve. And that's where the trap is.
(Note: If you haven't done so already, watch Video 2 to help you with the following entries.)

Distraction #1 (that I can't get rid off) is:

____

The payoff for keeping it is:

____

____

____

____

____

____

____

____

____

____

Distraction #2 (that I can't get rid off) is:

____

The payoff for keeping it is:

____

____

____

____

____

Distraction #3 (that I can't get rid off) is:

The payoff for keeping it is:

Final note on Day 1

This detox is creating the first dialogue between your Soul/True Self and your Persona. Do you have clarity on what's happening? Is it harder than you thought? Is it painful? What are you observing (psychologically, energetically, physically)?

DAY 2 - ENERGY

Welcome to Day 2! Today is a day of energy awareness. Eighteen hours of inner exploration.

So let's talk about energy, shall we?

Your energy reflects how deeply connected you are with your life on a spiritual level. The Soul's expression is energy.

Here's a quote from my book *You Are a Quest*:

> At a primal level,
> Reality is experienced through energy.
> Everything you think, say, or do
> Has a unique energy signature.
> Be aware of it.
> Expand it.
> Play with it.
> Project it.

Now I have a question for you: Have you ever had a moment in your life where someone told you what you wanted was "impossible," but you were so focused you did it anyway?

Of course! And maybe you were not aware that you ended up projecting high energy into your reality in order to bend it. As a human being, you are an energy being. Every time you enter a room and interact with others, your energy will dictate the quality of your experience and, most likely, your results.

Here, before we start, I'd like to make an important distinction between physical energy and spiritual energy. Physical energy is a gift that some people, including athletes such as dancers or boxers, are born with. And physical energy isn't evenly distributed throughout the population. It's true that you can reveal it, and later, dramatically increase it through training and good health habits (hint: don't smoke or drink), but it's highly unlikely that you'll become an athlete who can compete at the highest level if you're not gifted with this energy to begin with.

Next, there's spiritual energy. Spiritual energy is completely different, and that's what we're going to focus on here. It's a reflection of your Soul/True Self shining in the here and now. It's completely unrelated to your body: You can be injured, disabled, sick, or even on your deathbed, and yet display incredible spiritual energy.

The lives of saints and mystics are full of stories that show their incredible spiritual power. From their superior capacity for concentration, memory, vision, love, resistance to pain, or willpower, we see that mystics are connected to a source that defies our surface understanding of energy. This spiritual energy is what we'll be exploring today.

Yesterday we started our process by cutting away distractions. And removing distractions will cause an energy disruption with the Persona. This is done by design.

If it hasn't started already, know that your Persona is going to express itself through energy. Get ready for boredom, frustration, desire, anger—or all of the above! This is completely normal. And in this phase of the workshop, you're going to bring awareness to your energy levels.

So today I'd like to invite you to observe your energy levels throughout the day, for about eighteen hours (depending on how much you sleep), starting when you wake up, until the moment when you go to bed.

This is very easy: Set up an alarm that beeps every hour. Then, throughout the day, take a moment, every hour, to check in with yourself and assess your energy state.

Simply look at the energy chart below and write down the corresponding number, from the lowest, Apathy/Despair (00), to the highest, Equanimity/Oneness (10). Ideally you want level 05 to be your baseline.

We are going to do this monitoring for a week so you can discover which moments/situations are uplifting, and which are low energy.

ENERGY CHART

10 Equanimity/Oneness
09 Unconditional Love/Gratitude
08 Sustained Creativity
07 Enthusiasm/Inspiration
06 Curiosity
05 Self-Esteem/Confidence
04 Fleeting Happiness/Frustration
03 Anger
02 Fear
01 Grief/Guilt
00 Apathy/Despair

Here I'll show you an example, and I'll highlight peaks and lows with keywords describing specific moments. I invite you to do the same this week: Notice which moments have high/low energy and investigate to find out why, using the notes. Please continue checking in with yourself for seven days.

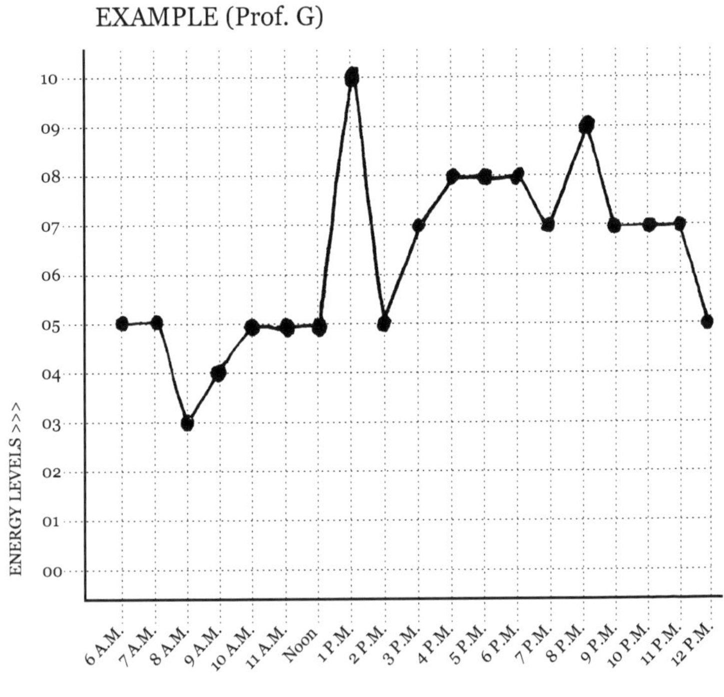

8 AM: Phone call w. car insurance wanting to raise premium → solved.

1 PM: Amazing blissful moment during the hike. So grateful to live in nature!

4 PM: Great writing session.

8 PM: Delicious dinner w. the Fam! ♡

9 PM: Watched "BARAKA" movie again amazing!

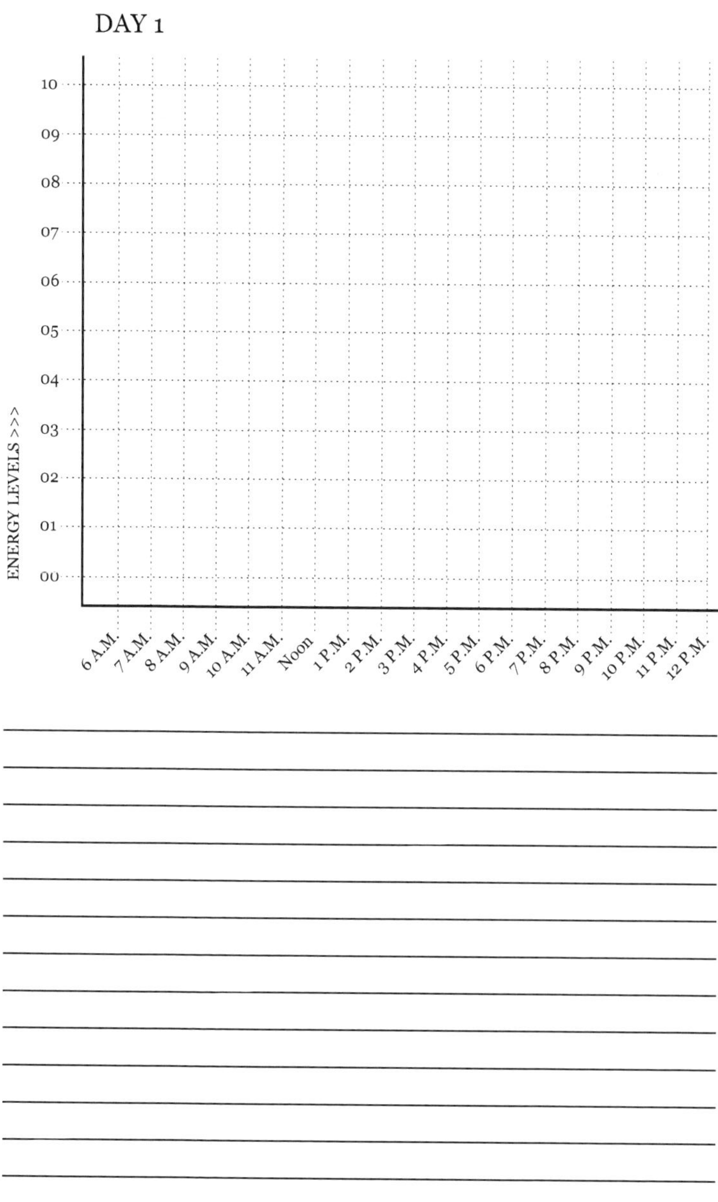
DAY 1
ENERGY LEVELS >>>
10
09
08
07
06
05
04
03
02
01
00
6 A.M.
7 A.M.
8 A.M.
9 A.M.
10 A.M.
11 A.M.
Noon
1 P.M.
2 P.M.
3 P.M.
4 P.M.
5 P.M.
6 P.M.
7 P.M.
8 P.M.
9 P.M.
10 P.M.
11 P.M.
12 P.M.

DAY 2

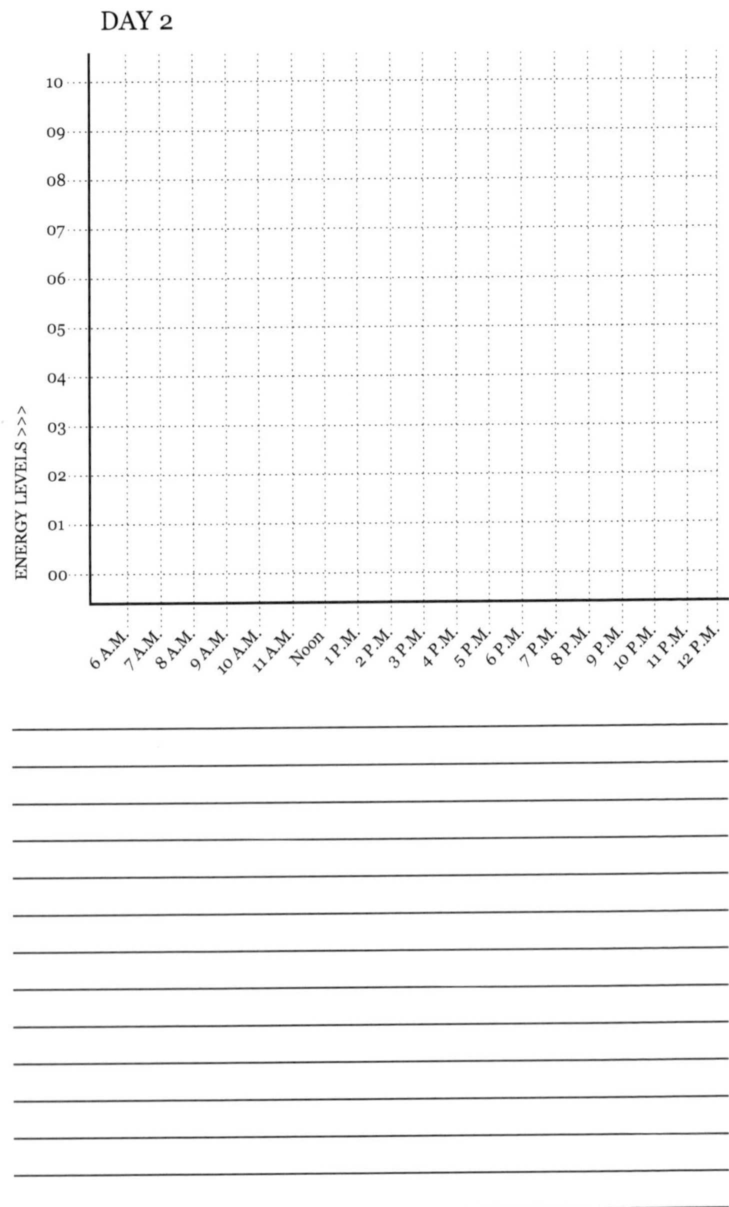

ENERGY LEVELS >>>
10
09
08
07
06
05
04
03
02
01
00
6 A.M.
7 A.M.
8 A.M.
9 A.M.
10 A.M.
11 A.M.
Noon
1 P.M.
2 P.M.
3 P.M.
4 P.M.
5 P.M.
6 P.M.
7 P.M.
8 P.M.
9 P.M.
10 P.M.
11 P.M.
12 P.M.

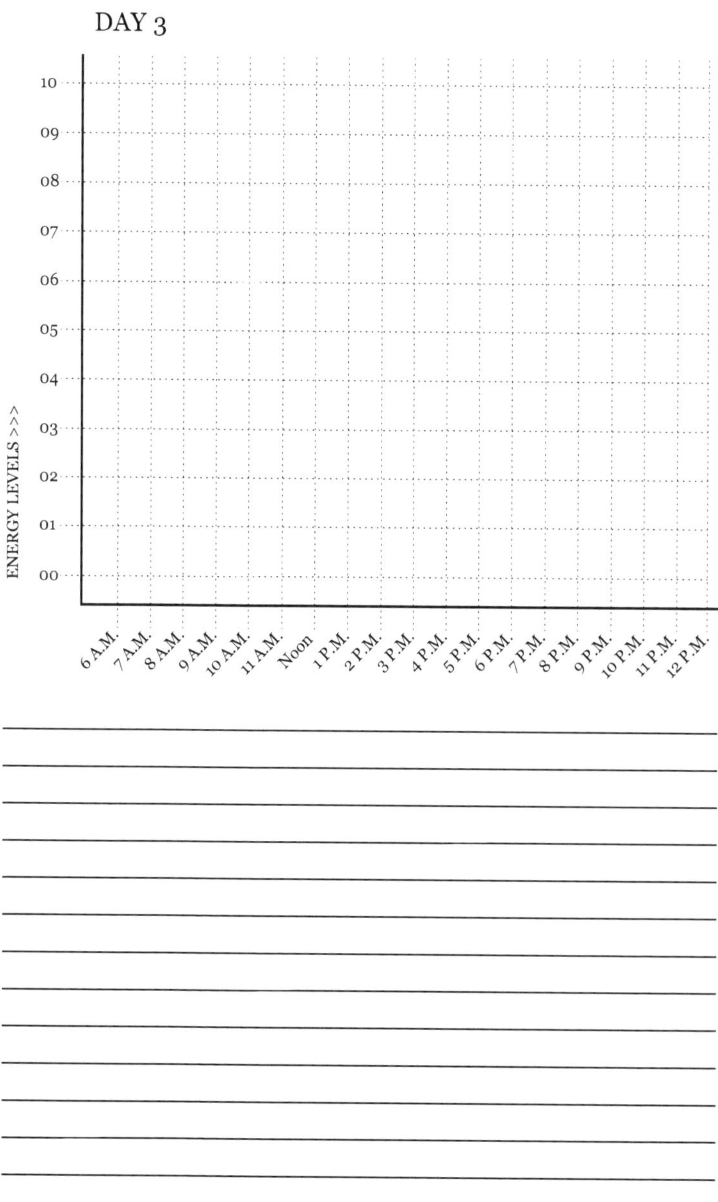
DAY 3
10
09
08
07
06
05
04
03
02
01
00
ENERGY LEVELS >>>
6 A.M.
7 A.M.
8 A.M.
9 A.M.
10 A.M.
11 A.M.
Noon
1 P.M.
2 P.M.
3 P.M.
4 P.M.
5 P.M.
6 P.M.
7 P.M.
8 P.M.
9 P.M.
10 P.M.
11 P.M.
12 P.M.

DAY 4

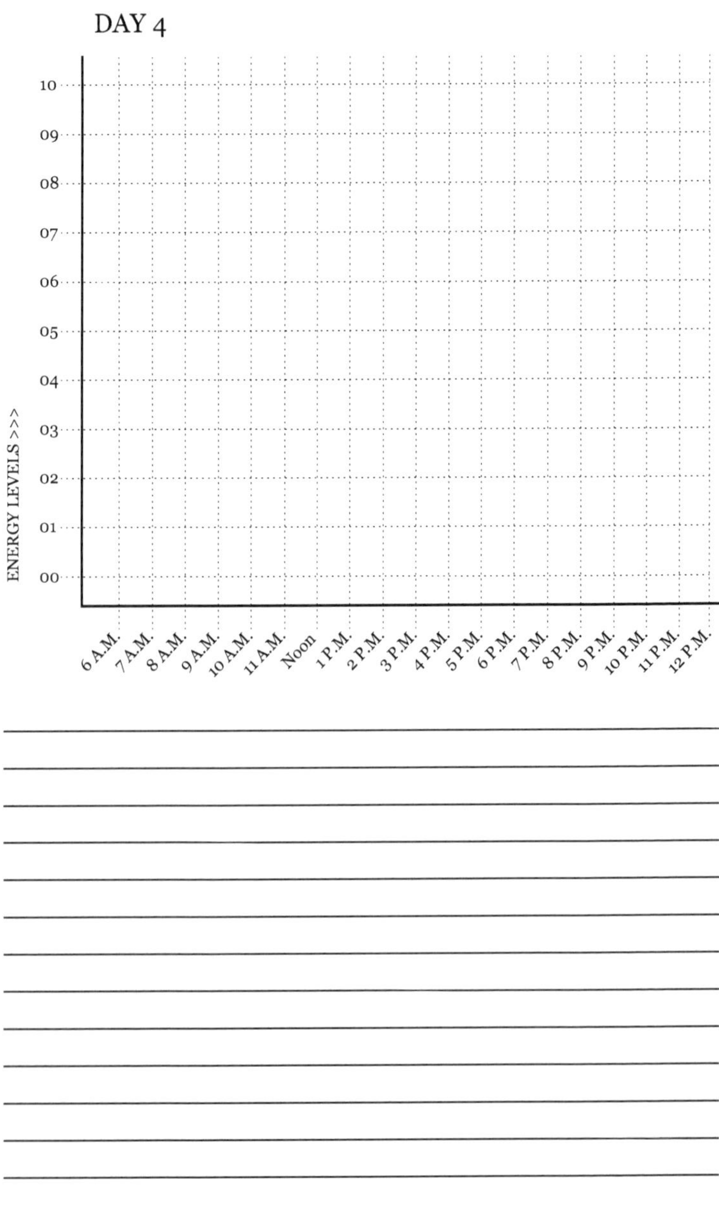
ENERGY LEVELS >>>
10
09
08
07
06
05
04
03
02
01
00
6 A.M.
7 A.M.
8 A.M.
9 A.M.
10 A.M.
11 A.M.
Noon
1 P.M.
2 P.M.
3 P.M.
4 P.M.
5 P.M.
6 P.M.
7 P.M.
8 P.M.
9 P.M.
10 P.M.
11 P.M.
12 P.M.

DAY 5

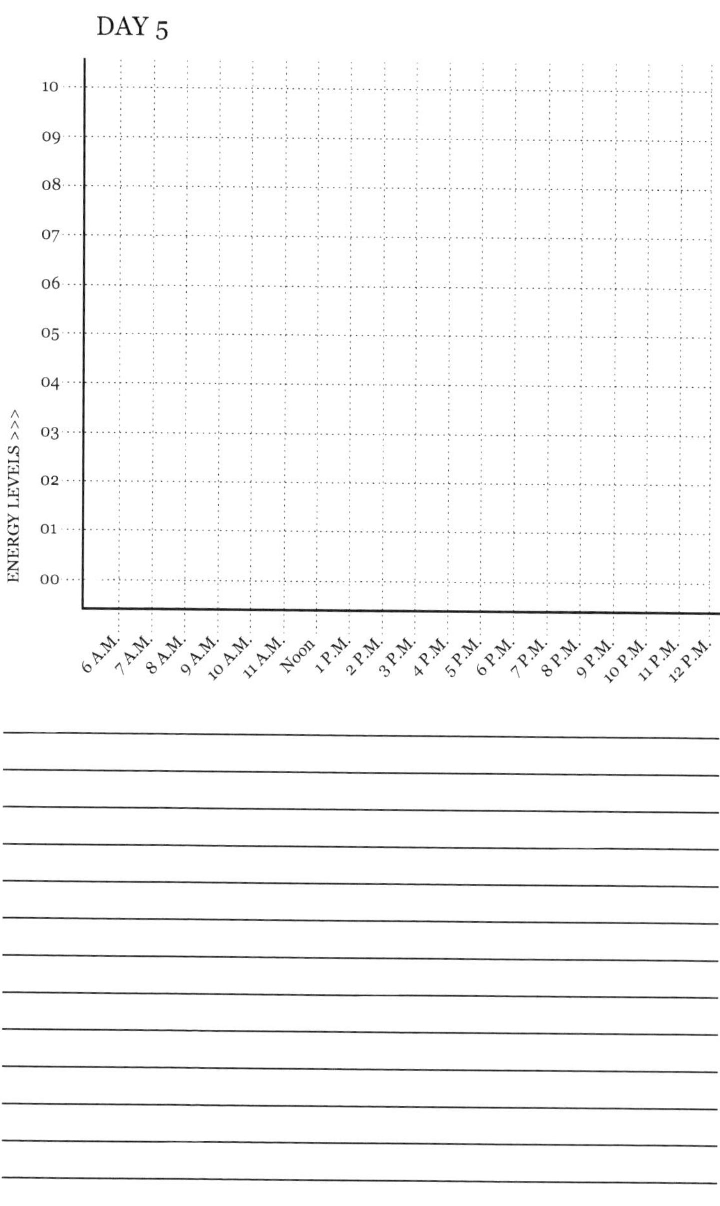
ENERGY LEVELS >>>
10
09
08
07
06
05
04
03
02
01
00
6 A.M.
7 A.M.
8 A.M.
9 A.M.
10 A.M.
11 A.M.
Noon
1 P.M.
2 P.M.
3 P.M.
4 P.M.
5 P.M.
6 P.M.
7 P.M.
8 P.M.
9 P.M.
10 P.M.
11 P.M.
12 P.M.

DAY 6

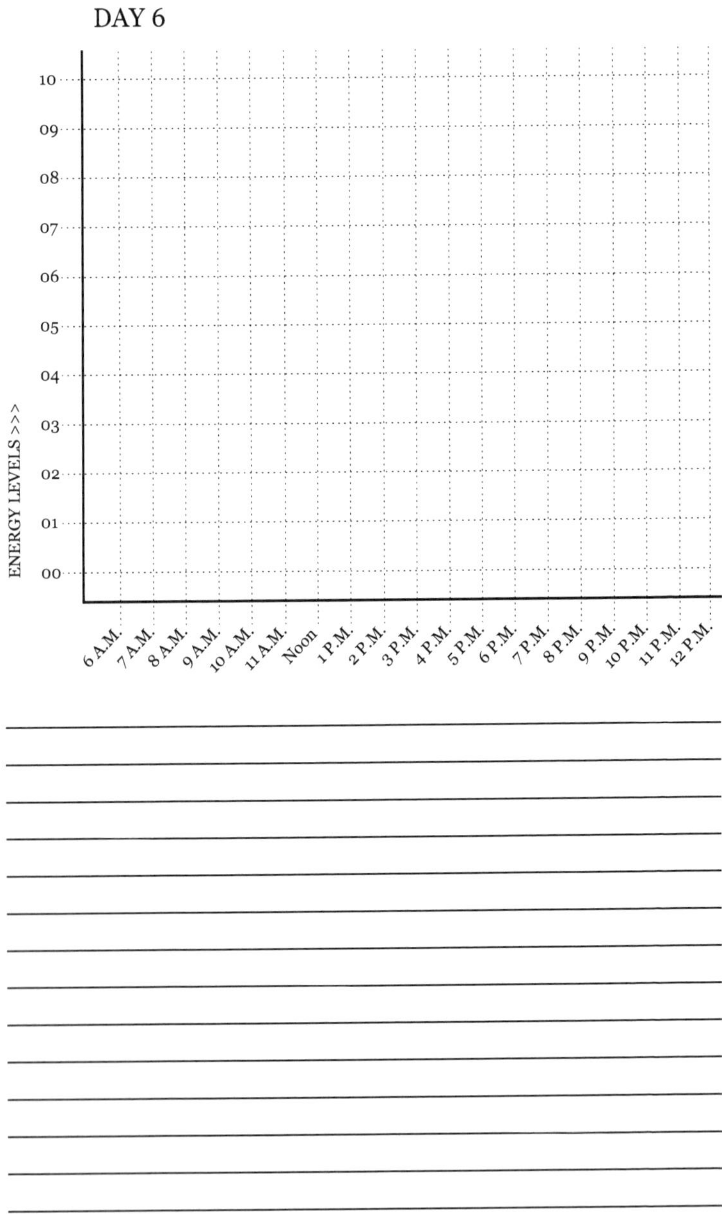
ENERGY LEVELS >>>
10
09
08
07
06
05
04
03
02
01
00
6 A.M.
7 A.M.
8 A.M.
9 A.M.
10 A.M.
11 A.M.
Noon
1 P.M.
2 P.M.
3 P.M.
4 P.M.
5 P.M.
6 P.M.
7 P.M.
8 P.M.
9 P.M.
10 P.M.
11 P.M.
12 P.M.

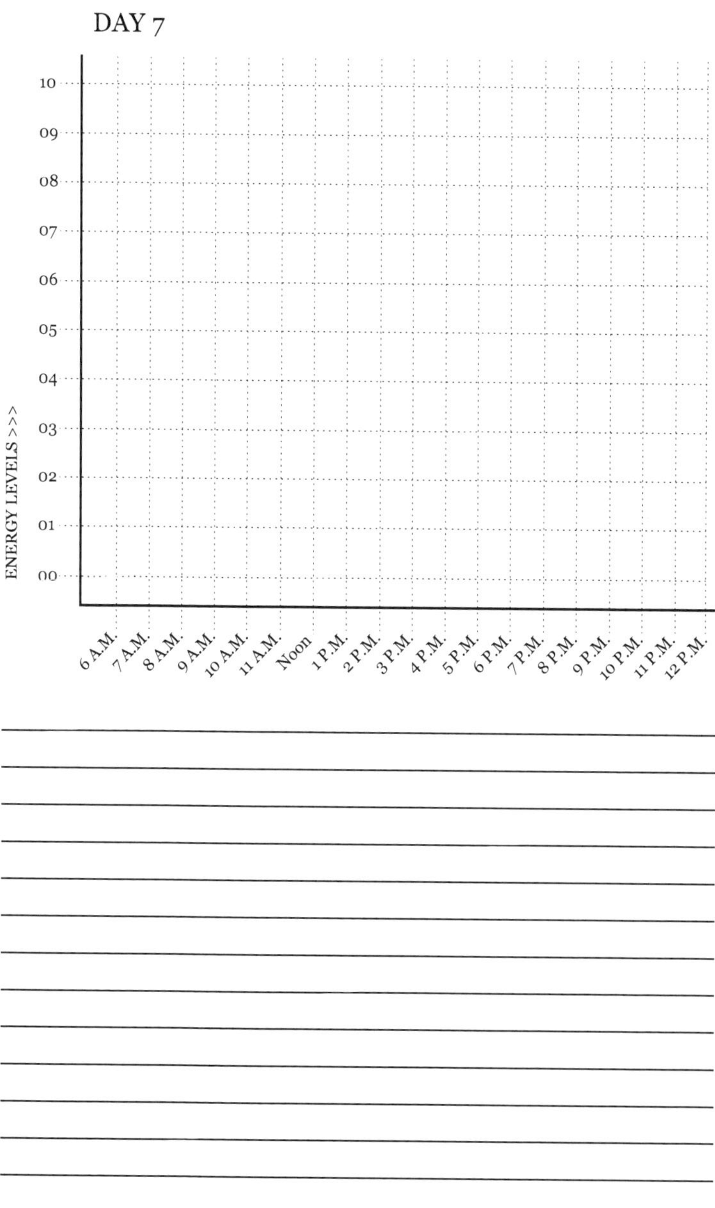
DAY 7
10
09
08
07
06
05
04
03
02
01
00
ENERGY LEVELS >>>
6 A.M.
7 A.M.
8 A.M.
9 A.M.
10 A.M.
11 A.M.
Noon
1 P.M.
2 P.M.
3 P.M.
4 P.M.
5 P.M.
6 P.M.
7 P.M.
8 P.M.
9 P.M.
10 P.M.
11 P.M.
12 P.M.

Here's a funny thing. This energy monitoring is obviously an exercise in awareness. And because energy flows where awareness goes, the more you monitor your energy states, the more you will move up the scale. How is this possible?

Because as you become curious about your energy levels through awareness, you're introducing intention into the experience.

Most of our energy states are happening in the background, on automatic, and we have little awareness of their movements. Once you start tracking your energy, you'll be more connected with it and you can become intentional. For example, if you notice that you're often at level 04: Fleeting Happiness/ Frustration, at some point you might ask yourself, "Why is that? Do I need to be there?" And if you realize that you are in this energy state thanks to the Persona, you'll find out that the true answer is "Of course not!" And suddenly, you can intentionally bump yourself up to level 05: Self-Esteem/Confidence.

Monitoring your energy is a great way to reveal your Soul power by discovering that your experience of life is self-directed by your awareness (or your lack of it) and your intention.

I'm going to give you a simple example.

As a teacher, I have a very big day during the week where I teach five hours in the morning, take one hour for lunch, teach another five hours in the afternoon, and at the end of the day, I have to drive back home for two hours. And, obviously, teaching demands a lot of energy if you want to keep your students engaged.

As you can imagine, this schedule is hard to keep up with.

In the beginning, I was at the same energy level of my students (low). But as I became more aware and intentional, I realized I could decide to raise my energy levels on command in order to raise the energy of my students in turn. And now, with practice, that's what I do—and it works great.

Awareness is transformative. Energy awareness combined with intention creates a super hyper transformative vibe!

But, concretely, how do you do it?

Let me show you.

. . .

BONUS: THE CIRCLE OF POWER

The circle of power is an energy exercise that traveled to us from ancient Egypt via the Greek mystery schools, and became a core practice of European alchemists and ceremonial magicians of the Renaissance. Now, I'd like to share with you the Reunion version, updated for today's world.

Here is how it works:

– Stand up in your room, or better, alone, in nature.
– First, do a quick assessment of how you are, energy-wise (from zero to ten).
– Imagine that there's a circle of light on the floor or ground, a few feet away from you.
– Be clear that this circle you are creating is a sacred space, where the power of the Infinite is reunited and flowing freely. This circle symbolically contains infinite energy.
– When you notice that your visualization feels almost real,

physically move your body into the circle of power.
– Stand in the middle of the circle, feet spread apart, hands on your hips (A.K.A. the Wonder Woman/Superman pose). Inhale deeply—and as you do, imagine being recharged by the infinite spiritual energy of the Creator, as you let go of all tension.
– Stay in the circle for about three to five minutes, focusing on feeling energy pouring through you.

Notice how your posture naturally improves as your body stands a little bit taller.
– Once you're done, step outside of the circle. Do a quick assessment of how you are, energy-wise.

Interesting, isn't it?

This is a powerful exercise. I recommend doing it every morning upon waking up. To learn more, please watch the next video.

 **WATCH VIDEO 2 ENERGY**

DAY 3 - REUNION (ASCEND/DESCEND)

Welcome to Day 3!
How are you doing? Is this workshop hard or easy?

Please write down your impressions here:

It's Day 3, and here's what's easy:

It's Day 3, and here's what's hard:

____

____

____

____

____

Today we're going to work on finding one aspect of your life where you'd like to see growth and transformation. And we're going to do it Reunion-style.

First, you need to pick a category from one of the domains of your life:

The Six Domains of Life

1. Self-expression/Exploration
2. Work and Finance
3. Health/Mind-Body
4. Relationships
5. Lifestyle/Art of Living
6. Purpose/Spiritual Life

Next, once you've selected one category, you are going to intentionally create change in it, in a dual movement: ascending and descending.

Let me explain.

- Ascending means a type of action that will elevate your Soul by letting go of the restrictions imposed by the Persona. This is done through learning, meditation, and visualization.

- Descending means a type of result-driven-action that just focuses on concretely creating change in the material world.

Bringing ascending and descending together is the foundation to create meaningful change in Reunion. It's the friction of these two opposite forces that lights up the fire of transformation. I'm going to give you a few examples now, so you get the idea:

Example A: Let's say that you are a freelancer and you chose 1. Self-expression/Exploration.

Here are possible ascending activities: Researching the culture of your field, analyzing business models, the background of the top players. Getting your sh*t together mentally and practicing action-without-action (in Daoism, a concept called Wei Wu Wei, 爲無爲), which means that you are going to learn to create or express yourself without the need to see immediate results, and without looking to get validation from others—this is action for the sake of the gesture itself.

Here are possible descending activities where you're looking to get results: Finalizing a project, and sharing it with your audience. Filming that damn YouTube video you've been talking about for the last six months. Writing a book. Making phone calls, writing e-mails, or showing up to an actual physical location to show someone what you do. Making a sales page on your website, etc.

Example B: Here's a real-life example of ascending/descending, connected with self-expression:

I've been self-publishing my own books for about ten years now, and I essentially work solo. Once I wrote, designed, and published my first book of the "You Are" series (*You Are a Circle*), I had the pleasure of seeing it available for sale on Amazon.com, and . . . nothing happened! To be honest, I was quite devastated, which seems completely ridiculous now because I actually thought that the book would sell by itself, magically! It did *not*. So I decided to go deeper. I practiced ascending/descending.

Ascending. I did a lot of inner work to learn to be okay with marketing and selling. I had so many blocks with it (thank you Persona)! So I picked up books about marketing and sales, and spent time visualizing myself not just being a creative, but also a small business owner responsible for promotion and sales. This is key: You become what you imagine yourself to be.

Descending. Next: action. I remember this day just like yesterday. I was going to the gym and I drove by a local store that would be a perfect retail space for my book. As I passed by, I felt a too-familiar sense of frustration, feeling disempowered. And, all of a sudden, this inner urge exploded from within: "*Enough! Stop the car!*" So I parked, and I visited the store in my gym clothes, with my book in hand. And here—I used to be so shy—I cannot even convey to you the dread I was feeling at that moment. I approached the store owner and simply said:

"Hi, I'm a local author and I wrote this little book that I feel could be a great fit for you. I'd like to give you this copy so you can check it out, and there's my info in the back if you're interested." And that was it.

Simple, right? Well, to me it was an incredible feat. But guess what happened? The store contacted me a few days later to ask for five copies. The week after that, they sold out and asked for five more. Then, another week later they asked for ten. And now, almost a decade later, this one little store has sold more than a thousand copies of my books and is still carrying them.

I'm sharing this story with you because ascending/descending is the key to everything. You absolutely need this dual movement to create deep, meaningful change. Depending on your personality type, you might be prone to either simply ascend or descend. But just focusing on one direction isn't enough.

And here, please make sure you look deep inside yourself to see which way the Persona is pushing you:

Are you deeply introverted, overanalyzing everything, and pushing away action? (Then you need to focus more on descending/action.)

Or:

Are you an extrovert, always running into action, but sometimes forgetting to "look before you leap?" (Then you need to focus more on ascending/visualization.)

Okay, so please pick a category:

The category I'm choosing from the six domains of life is:

____

____

____

Here's why it's important for me today:

____

____

____

____

____

____

If I don't make any progress in this category, ten years from now, I'll be:

If I successfully make positive change in this category, ten years from now, I'll be:

My ascending strategies are:

My descending strategies are:

Note: In our seven-day workshop I'm asking you to pick just one category to begin with so you don't get overwhelmed. Later, when you've become used to this process, you'll be able to work simultaneously on multiple categories. Work on this during this week, then come back to write down your results (positive and negative).

After working on this category for seven days, here are my observations and results:

Today, the video link is a guided meditation that you can listen to before going to bed. Check it out here:

 **WATCH VIDEO 3 REUNION**

DAY 4 - POSSIBILITIES (CREATIVE DREAMING)

Welcome to Day 4!
Congratulations, you are at the midpoint!

"What a feeling!"
(Yes, this is a reference to the classic eighties movie *Flashdance*—and the Irene Cara super song. If you know, you know.)

Speaking of which, how are you feeling today? What has been great so far? What has been hard?

____

____

____

____

____

____

____

____

____

____

____

____

____

____

____

____

____

____

____

____

Today we're going to explore possibilities—what I call "creative dreaming." As you've probably noticed by now, this book is the follow-up to my previous book, *You Are a Dream*, which talks about . . . creative dreaming! And because that book is 350 pages long, even if I quote from it here and there, I simply cannot condense it into one paragraph.

However, here's what we can do today: We're going to look at the most important aspect by exploring possibilities together.

So, here, we're going to use the six domains of life, and I'm going to walk you through a guided audio visualization to help you connect with the possibilities that are in your life right now. Simply find a quiet place, use your headphones, then, as you listen to the guided visualization, write down what comes up in the space below.

First, watch the video, and follow along with the book (see next page):

 **WATCH VIDEO 4 POSSIBILITIES**

The Six Domains of Life

As you watch video 5, write down your notes below:

1. Self-expression/Exploration

If you knew you could not fail, what would you create?

In what way would you grow? Who would you become?

Today, what's the first step you could take to move toward this new you?

2. Work and Finance

If you knew you could not fail, what would you create?

In what way would you grow? Who would you become?

Today, what's the first step you could take to move toward this new you?

3. Health/Mind-Body

If you knew you could not fail, what would you create?

In what way would you grow? Who would you become?

Today, what's the first step you could take to move toward this new you?

4. Relationships

If you knew you could not fail, what would you create?

In what way would you grow? Who would you become?

Today, what's the first step you could take to move toward this new you?

5. Lifestyle/Art of Living

If you knew you could not fail, what would you create?

In what way would you grow? Who would you become?

Today, what's the first step you could take to move toward this new you?

6. Purpose/Spiritual Life

If you knew you could not fail, what would you create?

In what way would you grow? Who would you become?

Today, what's the first step you could take to move toward this new you?

DAY 5 - EXPLORING THE CAVE

Welcome to Day 5!

How are you feeling today? What has been great so far? What has been hard?

Did you notice the Persona react through emotions, body sensation, or cunning little thoughts? Describe your experience:

Today, you're going to explore Plato's cave.

Plato's cave is the conditioned reality that keeps us trapped within the limitations of the Persona. This is done through a simple, but ruthless loop: Reality automatically creates a limited, conditioned self, the Persona; then, in turn, the Persona validates itself through reality. The cost is threefold: your freedom, the negation of your Soul/True Self, and the feeling of separateness (no unity).

In Reunion, because we're simultaneously ascending and descending, we're acknowledging that the consciousness of the Creator/God permeates every aspect of reality. Therefore, the illusion of Maya (Plato's cave), and its lovechild, the Persona, is really about the ignorance of oneness. In other words, reality is real, but our perception of reality and our "self" as duality/separateness is the illusion. In Eastern philosophies this idea is found in Tantra, and in the West it's a foundation of the mystery schools.

Now, you may ask, "How am I supposed to discover the illusion of Plato's cave while I'm in it, and while my sense of self is produced by it?"

Yes, the difficulty is real. As mentioned earlier, Plato's cave is an airtight prison.

So today, in order to explore Plato's cave, we are first going to explore it from the outside, and, very slowly, go back in.

. . .

Let's start outside, on a large scale. You are going to take a look at the way big entities such as corporations communicate and see if they are using the Persona language to keep you inside the cave.

For a jolly good time, you can start with advertising. Instead of being half asleep to the messages that are being bombarded into your mind 24/7, take a pause and bring full awareness to what you're being exposed to. Ask yourself these three questions:

"How is this message suggesting that I'm not enough?"

"Are they using emotions such as fear?"

"Are they associating an intangible quality with their product?"

If you do this exercise on a regular basis, you'll uncover that 99 percent of the messages you are being exposed to (advertising, or political) are designed to keep you deep inside Plato's cave. Do this exercise for a couple of years, and the game of the cave will become so transparent, you'll see it everywhere.

Today, I'm going to ask you to find three messages, and write down what you've found below. But before you start, I'll fill one out as an example.

(Note: This was an advertisement for a whitening strips brand from a few years ago.)

Brand: Whitening strips X

Story: In New York, two young women (who are friends) are taking a cab together.

Woman A: (speaking in a positive tone, suggesting hope for romantic love) "Hey, girl! Great news! I have a date next week!"

She's about to take a sip from her to-go coffee. Her friend stops her midpoint.

Woman B: (speaking in a condescending tone) "No, no! You don't want to ruin your smile! You *know* what happened last time!"

Woman A freezes. She looks embarrassed.

Woman B: (popping out a whitening strip from her handbag) "I have just the right thing for you! You're going to look great!"

Woman A: "Thanks, girl!"

(Product shot, end of commercial.)

Now let's analyze this message . . .

Q1: *How is this message suggesting that you're not enough?*
A: Here, it is implied that without supernaturally white teeth, you are not good enough to get a romantic partner.

Q2: *Are they using emotions such as fear?*
A: Yes! When woman B says: "You *know* what happened last time!" she rubs it in real well by suggesting that a potential lover ran away because her friend did not have a perfect smile at that time.

Q3: *Are they associating an intangible quality with their product?*
A: Yes! They actually go full on with it: Whitening strips equal being loved. Without the product? No love!

Interesting, isn't it?

Please look around and find three examples of brand messaging that use this type of approach. Write down your analysis of their message.

Name of Brand/Product #1:

____

____

Story:

____

____

____

____

____

____

____

____

____

____

____

Q1: How is this message suggesting that you're not enough?

Q2: Are they using emotions such as fear?

Q3: Are they associating an intangible quality with their product?

Name of Brand/Product #2:

Story:

Q1: How is this message suggesting that you're not enough?

Q2: Are they using emotions such as fear?

Q3: Are they associating an intangible quality with their product?

Name of Brand/Product #3:

Story:

Q1: How is this message suggesting that you're not enough?

Q2: Are they using emotions such as fear?

Q3: Are they associating an intangible quality with their product?

All right! This exercise is excellent training for beginners, because it's most likely that you have not associated your sense of identity with a specific brand (I sincerely hope so); therefore, these tricks are easy to spot.

Why are we talking about this in a book about spirituality? Simple: If you do not become an expert in understanding the messages that surround you, you will be controlled by them. Without clear awareness, you will be kept deep inside Plato's cave, and no book about spirituality (or teacher) will be able to get you out.

Once you start seeing these patterns in advertising messages (or social media), try looking at political messages as well (left or right) and you will find exactly the same tricks.

The next phase is to look at other people (friends, relatives, and coworkers) and simply try to spot when their Persona is acting through them. You can notice it when:

> - They need to change something about themselves by growing and evolving, but they state: "This is who I am. I cannot change." Or, the always hilarious, "This is impossible."
>
> - They behave in destructive ways, and as they do, they lose their sense of awareness (smoking, drinking, doing drugs, overeating, being addicted to social media or videogames, being addicted to porn, acting impulsively, etc.). Observe how they can always justify their actions with a twisted logic (because the Persona is a champion at justification).
>
> - They communicate in negative absolutes. For example: "I never get any lucky break!" "Society always brings me down," "I'm not good with business!" etc.

Important note: This exercise is about observation only. Do not attempt to "change" someone who's under the spell of the Persona, no matter how insane the rationalizations might be.

For example, if someone you know is a heavy smoker, avoid saying, “Stop smoking, you’re destroying your health!” It will never work. In this context, it’s much more potent to gently suggest, “I know there’s a side of you that’s more powerful than your smoking habit. I wonder what would happen if you started using your power?” And leave it there.

Here, you’re actually not talking to the Persona, but you’re planting a seed of possibility that’s directed at the Soul/ Higher Self. You’re asking this person to remember that he/she is more than just the Persona. And when, and only when, he/ she is ready to open up, change can occur.

If this is something that interests you, this approach to communication that involves talking directly to the Soul/ Higher Self is something we go into much more detail in the live Reunion workshops (see the end of this book).

Finally, you’re going to go inside, by learning to observe your thoughts. Looking into yourself—being self-reflective. This is the hardest part, of course; but if you make it like a game, it’s easier than you think. Try to catch the Persona when it’s acting out in your own life.

How?

Intentionally decide to experiment with activities that push you outside of your comfort zone. Create something new for yourself where there’s a learning curve, something where there’s a possibility for “failure” or, even better, embarrassment.

These are interesting examples:

- Are you a homebody? Sign up for a martial arts class.

- Are you shy? Salsa dancing class! Or (even better) try a public speaking class like Toastmasters.

- Urban dweller? Go camping!

- Extreme sports fan? Try meditating every morning. Simply focus on your breathing for five minutes. Observe as your thoughts arise, and let them pass. Focus again on your breathing. Once you've mastered this exercise, try ten minutes. Later, fifteen minutes.

- Your house is a mess? Watch some "how to clean your house" videos and start cleaning for fun.

You get the idea. By choosing to try something healthy that's outside of your comfort zone, you directly confront the Persona and force it to react. And when it does, simply write down what it says.

Let me give you an example. I used to have a student who was all brain and very disconnected from her emotions. So I challenged her to try salsa dancing. Do you know what her instant response was?

"Salsa dancing isn't going to change anything . . ."

This is an absolute. *Boom!* Gotcha, Persona!

You see, at this stage, you're just looking to trigger the Persona so you can learn how it operates in your own life. Don't judge it. Simply write down what it says.

Then simply ask: "How do you know this to be absolutely true?"

And when you're dealing with the Persona, who loves absolutes, this question is a killer. Because when it comes to the transformative power of dancing (or any other type of new activity that pushes you outside of your comfort zone), we simply don't know what's going to happen. And that's why it's great. You see, the Persona really wants for you to stay the same, so you never grow and evolve.

And guess what? Today, your Soul/True Self is traveling for a short time for an adventure called "your life" on this beautiful planet. As a Soul Being, you're here to celebrate growth, evolution, and change! And the more you challenge the Persona by exploring what's actually possible to be, do, and experience in your own life, the more you'll discover the incredible possibilities that are hidden in the present moment.

How do I know?

Let me tell you in our next video. In the meantime, go for it!

Choose a healthy activity that's outside of your comfort zone.

My activity is:

____

____

It's outside of my comfort zone because:

____

____

____

____

____

____

Reaction/comment from the Persona #1 (before the activity, just thinking about it):

Q: How do you know this is absolutely true?

Reaction/comment from the Persona #2 (during the activity):

WATCH VIDEO 5 EXPLORING THE CAVE

Notes:

DAY 6 - SURRENDERING INTO YOUR LIFE

Welcome to Day 6!

How are you feeling today? What has been great so far? What has been hard?

Did you notice the Persona react through emotions, body sensation, or cunning little thoughts? Describe your experience:

Today, you're going to look back into your personal history from the perspective of your Soul/True Self. As a human being living in this world full of duality, you have experienced many challenges, disappointments, and hardships. You have also experienced pure joy. These moments are part of the human condition and we're going to explore both.

First, I'm inviting you to write down five key challenging moments in your life, from your childhood to recent moments, and try to look at them from a higher perspective. Ask: "How was I able to go through this?" and "How did I grow from it?"

Challenging moment #1:

"How was I able to go through this?" and "How did I grow because of it?"

Challenging moment #2:

"How was I able to go through this?" and "How did I grow because of it?"

Challenging moment #3:

"How was I able to go through this?" and "How did I grow because of it?"

Challenging moment #4:

"How was I able to go through this?" and "How did I grow because of it?"

Challenging moment #5:

"How was I able to go through this?" and "How did I grow because of it?"

Next, look again into your personal history. Find five moments of pure joy. What did these experiences tell you about life?

Pure joy moment #1:

"What did this moment teach me about life?"

Pure joy moment #2:

"What did this moment teach me about life?"

Pure joy moment #3:

"What did this moment teach me about life?"

Pure joy moment #4:

"What did this moment teach me about life?"

Pure joy moment #5:

"What did this moment teach me about life?"

Now, after you've done writing down these personal history explorations, please stay in the moment. Check in with yourself. How do you feel right now?

I know this exercise isn't easy. Maybe you feel a flux of deep conflicting emotions that are hard to express. This is completely normal. And now I'd like to remind you of the Daoist symbol called Taiji (太極), showing the Yin-Yang symbols, two opposite forces, interlocked and dynamically joined in a dance.

This dance is your life.

That's why this exercise is so important. By revealing the challenges *and* the beauty in your life, you are centering yourself into your Soul's perspective.

When you're realizing that there's a dance, then you can become the dancer.

Notes:

DAY 7 - MEANING (SUPER HYPER VIBE)

The great spiritual adventure is the realization that you are a Soul taking a journey in this life, and being fully present in the world from that perspective.

On this last day, I'd like to invite you to spend time in nature (or find a park, if you live in a big city).

Once you're there, I want you to imagine this:

> Imagine, as you sit down in this peaceful natural environment that, all of a sudden, a great being of light appears in front of you. This magnificent, ethereal being has a unique energy signature that you recognize as angelic. In its presence, you feel pulsing waves of infinite love radiating toward you.
>
> The being says: "I'm here to bring you a message. I'm here to tell you that you are a Soul having a human experience." The being pauses for a moment and then adds, with a thundering voice: "You are the light! Feel your light! Shine your light!"
>
> There's a loud sound. And *poof!*—just like that—the mysterious being vanishes!

Now I really want you to internalize this story and consider it very seriously, as if it were real. Because if you want it to be, this can be more than just a story, but an initiatory myth to rejuvenate the experience of your own life.

Really consider it for a moment, then answer the following questions. If the story were real:

I would feel incredibly free and I would immediately stop hiding behind behaviors that no longer support me, such as:

Experiencing this infinite freedom, I would also be completely fearless and I would start:

I would be full of joy and love, and I would see myself as:

I would celebrate my infinite creative potential by:

I would bring meaning into every moment by:

Here are some final thoughts to end this workshop.

WATCH VIDEO 7 SUPER HYPER VIBE

Notes:

PART 4

GAME

CHANGERS

We've reached the last chapter of this book. And before I go, I'd like to leave you with some final thoughts.

In *Super Hyper Vibe!* my goal has been to show you that you can be a conqueror of your own life by switching from the struggle of the Persona to experiencing gratitude and love. Seeing that every single moment is a gift.

How?

By recognizing that you are a Soul having a human experience.

But now I'd like to invite you to play the game of your life by changing it.

What do I mean by that?

Early on in the book, I've hinted at the fact that reality doesn't exist in a vacuum but instead it is being shaped by how we engage with it.

Reality is not a fixed thing. Reality *is* elastic.

Interestingly, scientists are also telling us that our brain is constantly being changed by our thoughts and experiences. This is called "neuroplasticity." So there's an actual observable correlation between thoughts and biological change.

In that sense, inside or outside, thoughts (which lead to action) affect both ourselves and the world. As human beings, we are complex living systems interconnected with everything. Multitudes creating the One.

Through the workshop, I've created a context so you can experience this directly in just seven days. This is a great start, but what's next?

I'd like you to consider this question very seriously:

"As a Soul Being experiencing human life, in what way are you honoring the sacred in the now?"

This is the ultimate question that can change everything.

Because, yes, there's such a thing as the game of your life, and this game unfolds itself through spiritual living.

Now, connecting with this truth is not as easy as it sounds because the actual experience of life seems completely unspiritual. Just watch the news for an hour and you'll see. Reality brings so much friction.

But that's the illusion, *right there*. This friction is here for a purpose. It's here to awaken your Soul consciousness.

Living the spiritual life is like standing still in the eye of the storm. It requires complete clarity on the nature of the Soul. Not as an intellectual concept but as a direct experience (gnosis).

Once you're there, you can live your life with complete freedom, without fear, and win the game of your life by choosing how you'd like to play it. This is the reunion of heart (ascending) and will (descending), two opposites coming together as one.

Shine your light!
This book is just an introduction. There is so much more to the Reunion practice. It might take you some time to integrate some of these ideas, so feel free to digest them; then, later look back into the book and your notes.

So before we say goodbye, I want to leave you with this:

Bring full awareness to your present.
Experience your life from a place of possibilities.

And more important, know that:

You are the light!

And that your job is to:

Feel your light!
Shine your light!

This realization is the revelatory moment of unity that transforms your life—and therefore transforms all life. You see, if you've connected with the ideas I've shared with you in our time together, then perhaps, deep inside, you already knew all this all along, and reading this book has simply helped you remember who you truly are:

A Soul Being journeying in this space-time on our planet.

This is the first step.

This act of remembrance reveals the great Unity that permeates everything, the universal I AM, the Infinite Consciousness, simultaneously transcendent and immanent, living both in space-time and outside of time.

Love, joy, and play

I don't want to over-describe a moment that you should experience for yourself, but there is a curious joyful quality to realizing Unity. The Creator/God, as an emerging super-consciousness expressing itself through you, is doing it from a place of love, joy, and play.

And so should you.

If I were to ask a random crowd of people "How do you win the game of life?" I would probably get a mixed bag of answers with keywords like "courage," "hard work," "persistence," and "wit"—which are great qualities when you attempt to "win" a game.

But the spiritual game of your own life is no ordinary game. There's nothing to "win," because it's a game of becoming. Your life is an ongoing process of change and growth, and it's powered by the act of remembering that *you* are a Soul.

So this leads us instead to this very strange-sounding question:

"How do you become the game of your own life?"

To which I'll offer an even more enigmatic answer:

"Let your Soul be."

Again, coming from this perspective of love, joy, and play.

Here, there's nothing to add or explain, and I will let you meditate on it. But instead of trying to analyze with the Persona/mind, simply listen with your heart, and maybe something will arise. An inner smile. A memory of that little spark you've been looking for, for a very long time.

You are changing the world

As a teacher, I get asked questions all the time that have to do with finding purpose in one's life. As in:

"I'm stuck in a job I hate, my partner isn't very nice to me, and I know I have a lot of potential but I can't seem to be able to fulfill it."

Oddly, this is also a typical Persona statement.

Why?

First, this perspective is from the "me" (Persona) wanting something for itself. Next, instead of focusing on the only thing that counts—the present moment—we see that the person(a) is typically projecting into an imaginary future with a perfect outcome.

And as you can imagine, when you're trying to chase an imaginary perfect image (which can't be real), you will never get it. And, in a way, that's a good thing.

But simultaneously, I'm very aware that this question, hidden under this layer of the Persona, also implies the muffled call of the Soul looking for meaning.

Therefore, if you were to ask me the same question, I would say to you:

The purpose you're looking for is available *now*. Start where you are today, but instead of asking what good things you can bring into your life, simply ask yourself—as a Soul Being:

> "How can I contribute?"
>
> "How can I contribute to my work?"
>
> "How can I contribute to my relationships?"
>
> "How can I contribute to my health?"
>
> "How can I contribute to the world?"

You get the idea . . .

Here, *deciding* that you *can* contribute is a statement of infinite spiritual power and love wanting to be manifested in this reality. And the moment you shift to that perspective, you will discover that reality *will* reshuffle itself around you. How is that possible? Life wants to express itself through you. When you realize that you are a vessel for Life itself, you can open yourself up by letting go of your Persona, creating a space for Life to flow through you.

By letting go of everything, you will connect with everything.

Concretely, here's how it works: First, you will notice that all of your fears are baseless, and you'll move confidently toward your dreams. Next, you will stay completely unmoved when life tests you through failures, disappointments, and delays, because you'll integrate them as an important part of your journey. Or "alternative sources of energy," as one powerful Soul Being I know states it.

Because, as a Soul Being, you need to realize this:

You are unstoppable.

Your Soul vibrations (attitude, energy, and intent) are what create real, meaningful change, and, in turn, the reality you live in. You see, as you are today, you are already changing the world because, good or bad, you are deeply interconnected with it. *You are it.* Your vibrations are affecting everything and everyone. When your vibrations are Persona-based, reality freezes into the status quo. But when your vibrations are Soul-based, everything is open and possible.

And, today, if we had a live conversation together, I would also ask you to pay attention to two very powerful words (which are also enemies of the Persona).

These words are "inspiration" (which means, "in spirit"), and "enthusiasm" (which means "in God").

When you live your life from a place of inspiration *and* enthusiasm, you are living from the perspective of the Soul. You are an expression of it. And today, more than ever, that's what the world needs.

The world needs *you* to shine your light!

So shine on!

If only ten percent of the world's population were to live from a place of inspiration and enthusiasm, we would instantly enter a new era in the history of humanity.

Reality 2.0 would pop up right in front of our eyes.

Building the future that we want is possible. A future where we are reconnected with the Earth and each other is at our fingertips, because the future always starts *today*.

I hope you can join me in creating this Soul-based Reunion through love, joy, and play.

We can all come together to build it and nurture it, like a beautiful garden.

Are *you* coming?

Realize that beyond your Persona,
you are a Soul Being connected
with life and the Creator.
Live your life from this perspective.
This is where total spiritual freedom lives.

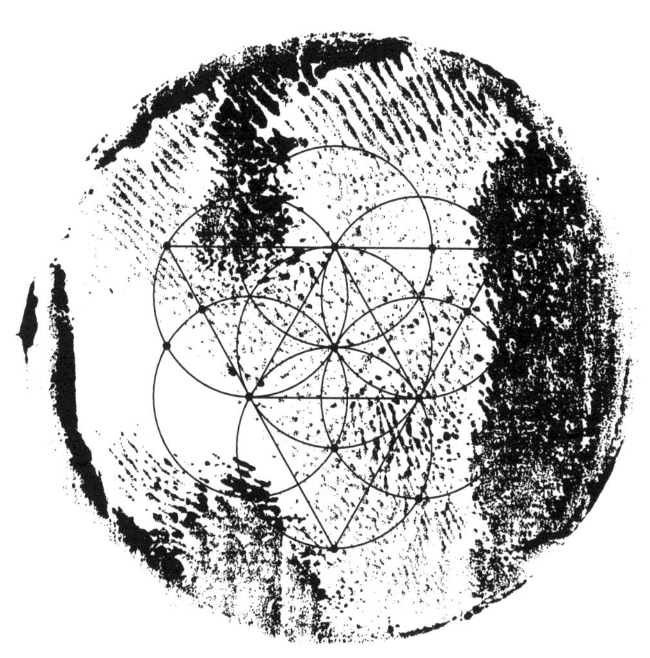

The present is immanence,
and immanence is the gateway into Infinity.
That's why being in the awareness of the Now
is the most important skill you can cultivate.

Reality is not a fixed thing.
Reality *is* elastic.

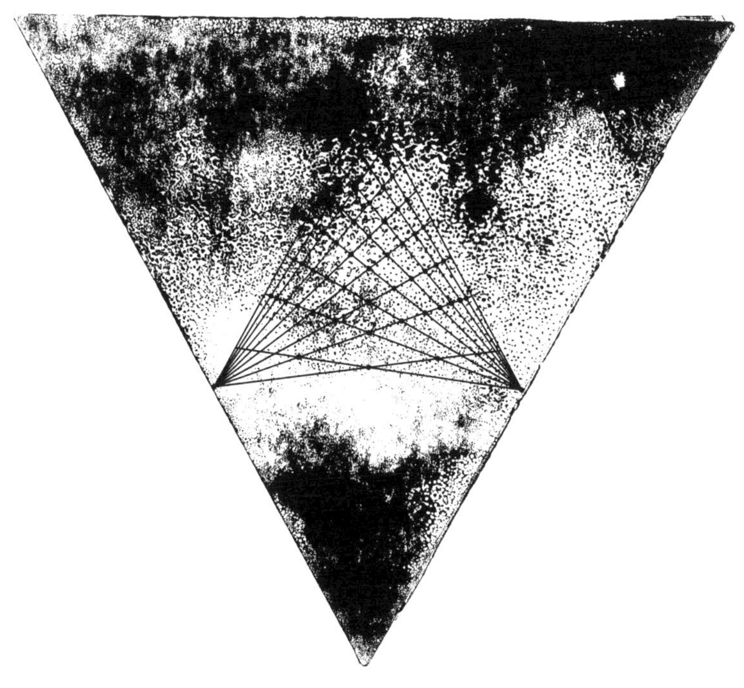

There is a curious joyful quality to realizing Unity. The Creator/God, as an emerging superconsciousness expressing itself through you, is doing it from a place of love, joy, and play.

Deciding that you *can* contribute is a statement of infinite spiritual power and love wanting to be manifested in this reality. And the moment you shift to that perspective, you will discover that reality *will* reshuffle itself around you.

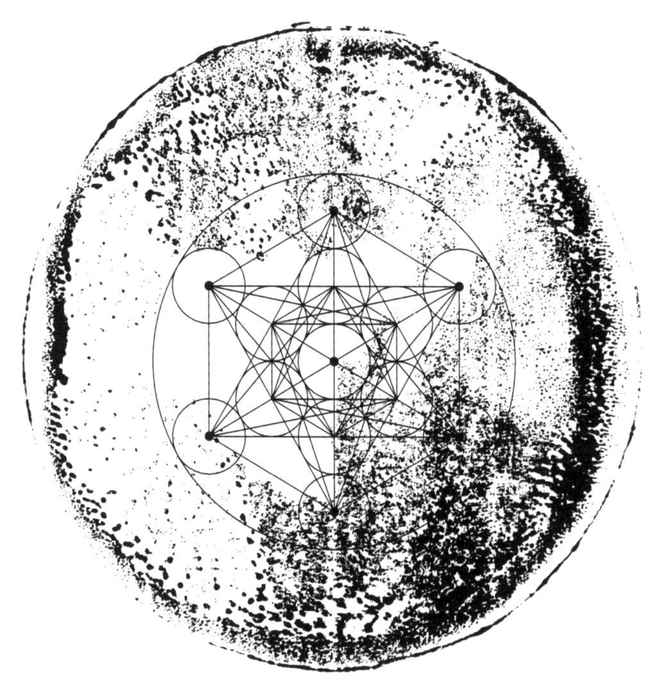

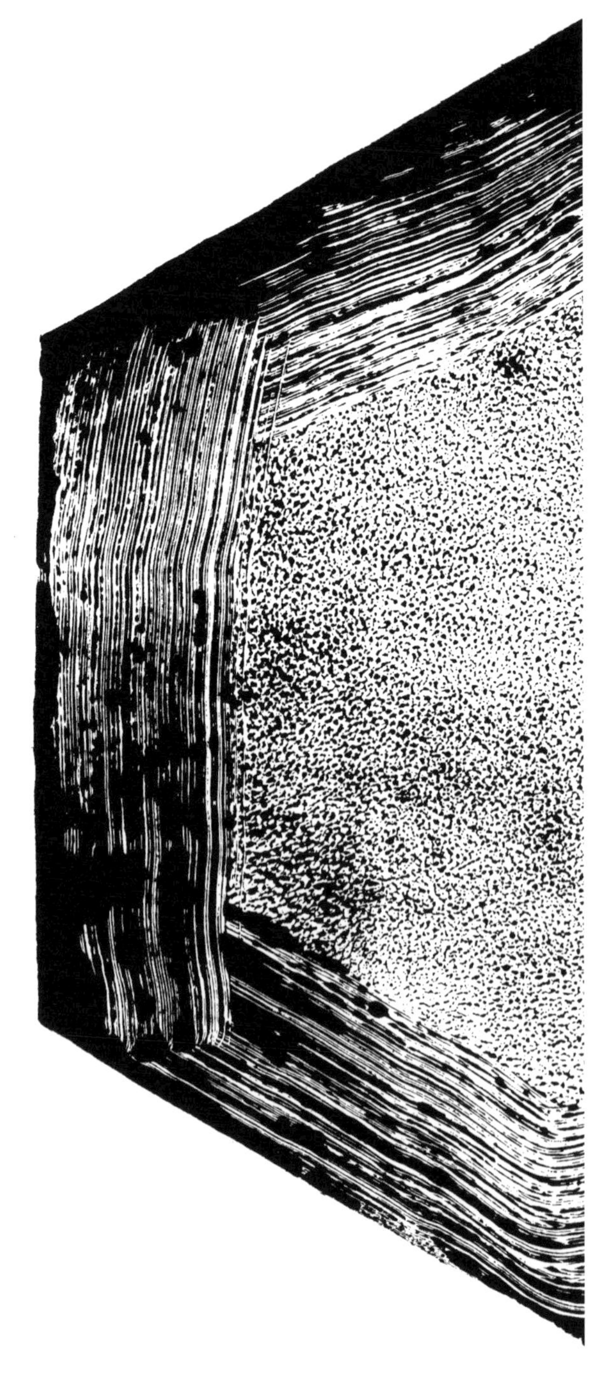

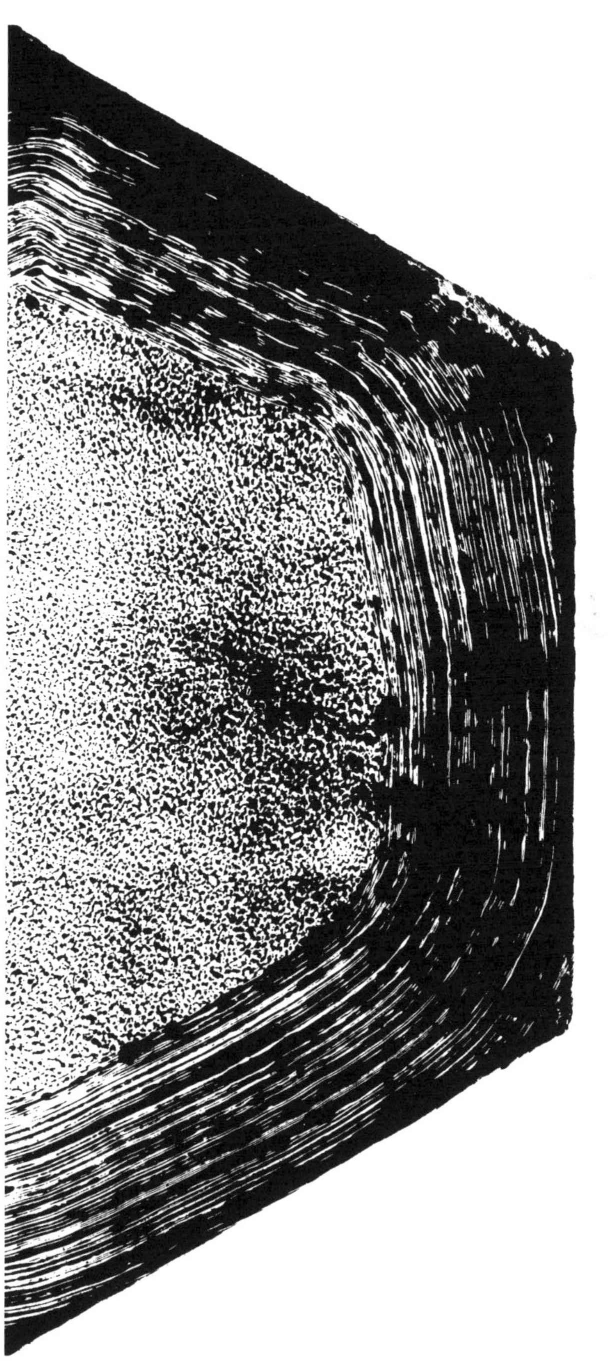

Notes:

RECOMMENDED

- Campbell, Joseph, *Man and Time*, 1957, Princeton University Press.
- Campbell, Joseph, *The Hero with a Thousand Faces*, 1949, Princeton University Press.
- Dass, Ram, *Be Here Now*, 1971, Lama Foundation.
- Dyczkowski, Mark, *The Aphorisms of Śiva*, 1992, SUNY Press.
- Jung, Carl Gustav, *Man and His Symbols*, 1968, Dell.
- Krishnamurti, Jiddu, *The Future is Now*, 1989, Harper & Row.
- May, Rollo, *The Cry for Myth*, 1991, Norton.
- Meyer, Marvin; Pagels, Elaine, *The Nag Hammadi Scriptures*, 2009, HarperOne.
- Pagels, Elaine, *The Gnostic Gospels*, 1989, Vintage Books.
- Talbot, Michael, *The Holographic Universe*, 2011, Harper Perennial.
- Teilhard De Chardin, Pierre, *The Phenomenon of Man*, 1976, Harper Perennial.
- Watts, Alan, *The book on the taboo against knowing who you are*, 1999, Random House.
- Watts, Alan, *This is it*, 1973, Vintage Books.

Favorite movie

Baraka (1992), directed by Ron Fricke.

About the guru game

Kramer, Joel; Alstad, Diana, *The Guru Papers: Masks of Authoritarian Power*, 1993, Frog Books.

Documentary: *Wild Wild Country* (2018), TV Mini-Series directed by Chapman and Maclain Way, Netflix.

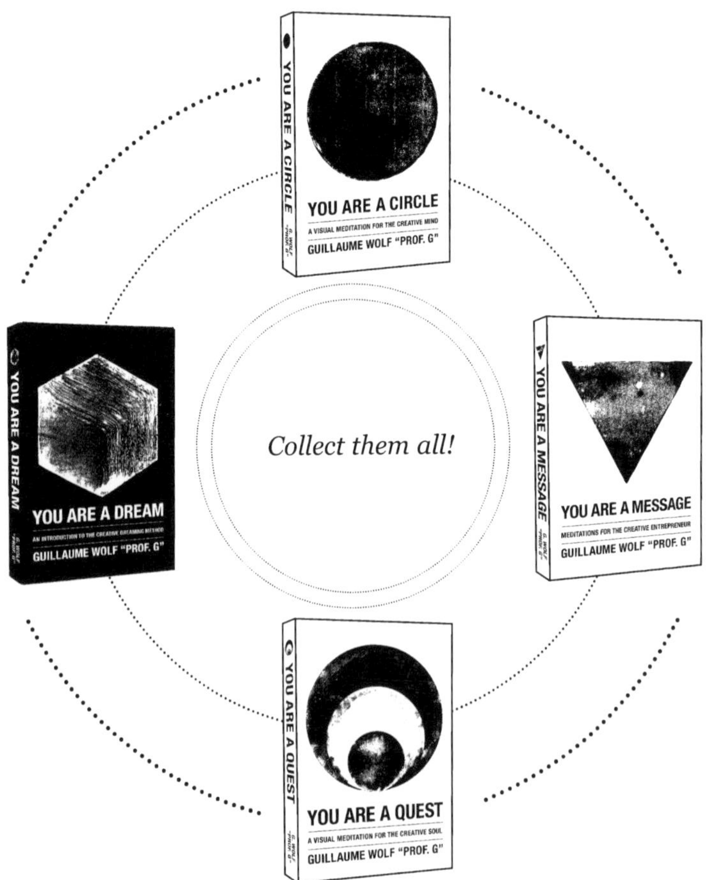
YOU ARE A CIRCLE
A VISUAL MEDITATION FOR THE CREATIVE MIND
GUILLAUME WOLF "PROF. G"
YOU ARE A DREAM
GUILLAUME WOLF "PROF. G"
Collect them all!
YOU ARE A MESSAGE
MEDITATIONS FOR THE CREATIVE ENTREPRENEUR
GUILLAUME WOLF "PROF. G"
YOU ARE A QUEST
A VISUAL MEDITATION FOR THE CREATIVE SOUL
GUILLAUME WOLF "PROF. G"

"GET INVOLVED!"

Hello, friend,

I hope you've enjoyed exploring this book and that it will inspire you to go out there and do great things.

This book and its companions are an experiment in publishing: It's a labor of love.

So if you really like this book and want to see more in the future, *get involved!* Please join me in this adventure by supporting it.

What you can do:
Please post about this book on your social media platform:
Use **#SuperHyperVibe**
and you can also tag me on

Instagram **@profG.co**
TikTok **@profG.co**
YouTube: **@profGshow**

Please leave a review on **Amazon.com** and share your story about how this book is a part of your life. It really helps, and it's super-nice to hear from you.

I really appreciate your support.

Guillaume "Prof. G"

GO DEEPER: REUNION WORKSHOP

Inspired? What's next?

This book is an invitation to reflect and explore, to open new doors. But there's more . . .

If you're curious about joining "Prof. G" for a live event, simply visit:

www.profg.co/reunion

ABOUT THE AUTHOR

Author, teacher, and spirituality explorer Guillaume Wolf "Prof. G" helps you dream big dreams, and make them real.

Through his books and online courses, Prof. G's mission is to empower, inspire, and challenge creatives of all walks of life to use their creative skills to bring meaningful change in their lives and make a positive impact in the world.

Prof. G is an associate professor at ArtCenter College of Design in Pasadena, California, where he teaches communication design and the psychology of change.

www.ProfG.co

Printed in Poland
by Amazon Fulfillment
Poland Sp. z o.o., Wrocław

62159097R00153